TRANSITIONS

Accounts of the Soul's Journey

GUINEVERE MASSEE

Introduction by Marilene Isaacs

BOATSWAIN PIPE PRESS

ISBN-10: 0615570666
ISBN-13: 978-0615570662

LCCN: 2012935588
Boatswain Pipe Press
United States

Dedication

For Jay; you gave me hope in a dark time and helped to realize that true happiness is possible if we choose to accept it.

Table of Contents

Introduction

I am pleased to write an introduction for this amazing book *Transitions: Accounts of the Soul's Journey*. It is refreshing to see such a wide array of experiences and ways of raising consciousness in one body of material. This book is a huge departure from the normal "New Age" books that say little and are a repeating of information. This book covers a wide range of situations and experiences of Souls after they leave this plane of existence. The healing aspect for the author is that she figures out what her nightmares are about and instead of staying stuck in fear, she pursues and breaks through the veil into the realization that she is in direct contact with those on the Other Side. These souls want their stories told so that we can all learn from their personal experiences on Earth and the Other Side.

I love how subjective reality and higher consciousness morph and healing manifests in the lives of the Souls who have stepped forward. This is an interesting read as it is truly based on Guinevere's unique connections through dreams as a conduit by which these Souls have spoken. This book is a great reminder to be here now...in Present Time...as Spirit always says to me "this is not the dress rehearsal, or the trial run, this is it!" When you read these stories, you will realize how easy it is to learn your lessons here on Earth.

We live in an amazing time on Earth where Spirit is communicating and people, such as the author, are listening. It is a time I have long awaited. I have been doing my Spiritual Work for many lifetimes. I am a Spiritual Teacher as well as an intuitive healer for people, animals and places. I have been completing this work for 42 years. I assist people in their journey by showing them that they do not have to learn out of suffering and the repeating of patterns. I personally know the author of this book and she has come to me several times for assistance; she is a remarkable young woman and has a unique talent in the Spiritual Realm that I am happy to see is manifested here in this book.

There is no death; it is like walking from one room to another. The greatest truth of all is that Love Never Dies. Life and death and all of our experiences lead us to the Actualization of Unconditional Love for self and others...it is not just a concept. Those who have open eyes to see and clear ears to hear will resonate with this book. Reading this book has inspired me to finish the writing of a couple of books that I have been working on for over 30 years. I'm certain you will be seeing more from me and Guinevere in the future...sending love and healing to all. Marilene Isaacs

Note from the Author

I was driving my old convertible one morning in 2009 with the top down on my way to work. It was a perfect summer seventy-six degrees. I was stopped at a red light and happened to look beyond it, up at the clouds traveling briskly along to some distant unknown destination. It was one of those days when the clouds are large and white and very fluffy, casting random shadows on the ground.

I thought about the light and shadows and how experiencing each was necessary in order to have a full appreciation of both. I drove under intermittent warm sunshine and cool shade and it was a pleasant drive for the most part. An idea began to form that maybe life was like my morning drive; mostly pleasant even with shifting circumstances. However, the idea changed somewhat after I drove under a cloud whose shadow seemingly followed me and left me shivering.

What happens if we have difficulty finding our way out from under a shadow; how then to move on into sunshine? Do we wait for the cloud to pass? The epiphany I experienced is that we have to choose to seek out the light. We cannot control our circumstances, yet we can control how we respond to them.

This experience gave me inspiration to write the book *Transitions: Accounts of the Soul's Journey.* I had been keeping a daily journal and dream notebook from 2005 which had the purpose to help me cope with terrible nightmares with which I had been plagued. As I discovered, the purpose of the journal was far greater than I had imagined.

Transitions: Accounts of the Soul's Journey is a book with the objective of opening the mind and considering life and death from different viewpoints. The stories contained within are from a great many different voices. I communicated with souls that were from the remote past, recent present and distant future, as well as a few that seemed to have no time association whatsoever. Some have asked for assistance and a few just want to be remembered. Each one has a very personal message to convey through their story. It is my fondest hope that you will gain insight, make a connection, know you are not alone and feel empowered to make better choices.

Sometimes it takes a big event, a "kick" of sorts in order to get us moving out from under the cloud towards the sunshine. So it is in life; why would it be any different in death? What if the "kick" sometimes happens to *be* death? I am proposing that we can still learn after we die; indeed, I am saying that sometimes we must in order to progress.

Please note that I have changed names and kept locations confidential in order to protect the identity of the families of those listed in this book. The dates shown will be within five years before or five years after the date listed so that you will have an idea of the timeframe for each story.

For some, the stories are not finished and you may feel compelled to contact me with further information. I welcome your participation and look forward to hearing from you. Please contact me at Guinevere@ GuinevereMassee.com or visit me at www.GuinevereMassee.com.

1

Messages From The Distant Past

Listen and Think for Yourself

How many times do you dream, wake up thinking about it but simply write it off as folly? Don't be too hasty. The unconscious mind notices subtleties that we do not. It draws connections between things we cannot, in our realities, connect. The logical side of our brain often causes us much trouble as we try to open the realm of possibilities and ideas that we do not fully understand. Surely there are some things that cannot be exactly or logically explained, yet somehow they "feel" right within us.

Many times our unconscious mind communicates with us through dreams – and many of the ideas that we consider impossible or wrong are shown to us differently…creating possibilities we never thought existed. Though our head may not understand or agree, our hearts may be a better compass for our decision making process.

This chapter contains stories with messages that get us more in touch with the unconscious things we do or have done that affect our current daily lives. Why do we hold certain values or beliefs? Can we attribute everything we are to this one current life we are living now? Do we only get one chance to get it right?

The answers, ultimately, depend on you and your willingness or unwillingness to really listen and think for you. Can you get beyond the parameters set up by hundreds or even thousands of years of human incarnation and rule-making on the planet? In the end, you have the choice to decide what is right for you regardless of the current socio-economic or religious systems in place. Just by asking simple questions you open up possibilities. Understand that by making no choice you are still making a choice.

Pay attention to your dreams. Think about what you could learn by watching your dream unfold. Understand that there are influences beyond our understanding accepting that your brain may fight it while your heart may know and embrace it. The choice is always yours.

Tundra Woman

Prehistoric Time in a Far North Country (North America)

The Tundra Woman came to me in a dream time and again over a period of six months. I watched the scene unfold each time, until finally, I wrote it down on October 20, 2005. After I wrote it down, she did not come to me again.

I was allowed the observation, and though the Tundra Woman does not speak directly, she is aware of my presence – indeed had sought it out. Thus the account is described below.

Listen to Your Dreams

It always began in darkness; comforting, surrounding, enfolding. The blue-black sky went on forever, meeting the edge of the world in a snowy, windswept plain. The cold embraced her, loving every bit of her exposed skin. She allowed it; no, she was grateful for it. She let the fur-lined parka hood fall to her shoulders. She breathed the cold air into her lungs, welcoming the sensation of being alive. The wind gathered her long dark hair in icy hands and pulled it behind, tugging gently at the tips. Her almond shaped eyes surveyed the landscape. White snow lay for as far as she could see.

She went forth across the fair snow, the crunch sounding softly beneath her fur-wrapped feet. She had come from far away to meet someone. She had come because of a dream. She listened to her dreams.

She slowed and paused. It was the place of her dream, utterly silent. She waited, filled with anticipation. She cupped her hands to her mouth, raised her head and called out into the night. She expected an answer. She was not disappointed.

From somewhere in the night, a lone voice replied. A howl pierced the silence. It was not a mournful cry as one might have expected, but a powerful appeal for the pack to come together. The woman cupped her hands again and called into the wind, asking for what she did not know; only knowing that she had seen this before - and she knew what awaited her.

They came, padding on light feet, like shadows moving swiftly between the known and unknown realms of the earth. Shadow forms created by a bright moon shifted and changed as they drew closer. One form grew larger while the others waited at length. The woman kneeled down, rocking back on her heels. The beating of her heart thumped loud enough for the pack to hear.

The great silver-white wolf came fully into view. Her long legs and trim body revealed a tall graceful appearance. Her muzzle was narrow and elongated; features punctuated by piercing yellow eyes that conveyed vast intelligence. She was striking. She was the most beautiful creature the woman had ever seen.

But there was more to this lovely creature- more and the woman knew this to be true. The silver wolf's countenance proclaimed it with every movement. She went to the woman and nuzzled her face gently, her wet nose sending shivers down the woman's spine. The wolf turned to the others and called them forth. It was a homecoming; a reunion of hearts and souls. The woman was greeted in a blur by all of them in turn- and they were not strangers. She enjoyed watching the frolicking play unfold before her.

The great silver wolf alone sat next to her. She looked profoundly into the woman's dark brown eyes. A deep bond connected them together- an ancient tie, an unknowable link in the conscious mind, buried in the unfathomable depths of the subconscious where only past life memories and knowledge of the Other Side are kept under spiritual lock and key.

The woman draped her arms around the wolf's neck and buried her face in the soft fur. She was safe. She was home. She was loved and accepted. The great wolf laid her head on the woman's shoulder. In a moment, the woman was asleep. She would awake in the morning, yet again, to the memory of the great silver wolf and her wolf family.

She would dream the next night and anticipate the next gathering.

Melissa

480 BC at a Temple in Brauron (Greece)

The girl was laughing and walking with another girl, in my dream, and both were adorned with crowns of leaves. Flowers had been woven through their long hair. They wore sleeveless saffron-colored tunics and were barefoot. There was merry music being played somewhere close and the smell of roasting meat wafting in the air. It was a celebration.

I saw behind her, an altar, bloody from sacrifice. It was then that I noticed her bare upper arms, marked with the blood of the great white ox that still lay there being butchered. It was an honor. She was being honored, as were other young girls her age.

Her name was Melissa.

I discontinued my spirit viewing and became part of the crowd watching the rite, standing very near to her. When the girl called Melissa looked my way I caught a reflection of myself in her eyes. I felt she would not die that day; that was not the purpose of her visit. She had come to tell me a story. She turned and beckoned me to follow and I did.

Her story, for me, is a fantastic look at strength, courage and love; it follows below and is written in Melissa's own words. I woke on the morning of April 22, 2009 to blue, cloudless skies.

Respect Conveyance

I felt his gaze before I actually saw him. I waited a moment before looking up discreetly to see that he stood slightly apart from the crowd of people that had gathered to watch the procession in which I walked. He was tall and lean, very tan from days spent in the sun.

He was definitely a soldier, and from his age and demeanor, a high-ranking officer. His faded brown hair was tied back, exposing the line of his jaw, following to a long, thin vertical scar on his neck. Even at my 15 years of age and complete innocence, I knew him to be desirable. I knew, also, the fire that smoldered in his dark eyes as he gazed at me; he knew of passion and indeed, I felt ignited.

Though there were throngs of people crowding to witness the procession, there were only the two of us sharing a private moment; a connection somehow. I smiled inwardly, glanced down at the bouquet of white flowers surrounding the honey that I carried and slipped one to the ground as I walked by him.

{Melissa was smitten, for sure, but she also understood that I didn't have the background that I needed in order to understand what I had seen thus far. We visited over the course of many weeks so that I could write down, very specifically, her story and understand the culture guiding it.}

We were numbered thirteen, all of us young maidens of noble birth, and we were leaving the sanctuary of the Goddess Artemis' temple. The temple had been my home from the time that I turned three years old. I had been chosen to learn the Great She-Bear's mysteries and ways; yet, we cannot stay forever in her arms. Artemis had called me to her, and yet, I had stayed longer than most and it was time to leave. It was a day to be remembered. It was the morning of the Arkteia Ceremony.

Early spring had breezed in and peppered our dry lands with colorful little flowers. A wind as slight as a breath kissed my skin. The cobblestone was warm and comforting beneath my bare feet. Fine tan dust felt like powder between my toes. With saffron-colored robes and green leafy crowns upon our heads, we were to become the Bear, to be wild before we were domesticated in marriage. This was how we would appease our goddess Artemis, Lady of All Animals Wild.

The white flowers I carried symbolized virginal purity, the honey signified the sweetness of life brought from communal work and sacrifice. These were to be gifted to Artemis on her many altars at Brauron. Other girls carried the gifts of spindles, cloth, incense, grain and weavings. Finally, we would offer her the blood of one perfect white ox.

We had started our journey from the sanctuary Acropolis in Athens and made our way with long procession to Artemis' sanctuary temple at Brauron. We were to offer a ritual Arkteia as we prepared ourselves for marriage and children. No man of any standing would marry a woman who had not taken part in this rite or had representation in this ritual. This festival procession happened every four years with wide attendance, yet we were only allowed to participate once, and it marked our leaving.

Late in the day, we crossed a rutted stone bridge over a narrow river, walked past a sacred spring and finally into a courtyard. The temple itself was intimate, yet the grounds would accommodate hundreds of people. From the courtyard, we approached a slightly raised stone altar, though there were many smaller altars specific for the gifts we had brought.

We rested awhile and took refreshment. Races had been set up for the younger girls from our temple in honor of the chase; Artemis enjoyed the hunt and especially the chase. When these were completed, we were asked to place our gifts to Artemis on their proper altars. After placing my gift and saying a prayer we went to the main altar and kneeled.

We paid no attention to the crowd. We came only to pay homage to our goddess and placate her with our gifts and dancing. Artemis was a virgin goddess; for many of us, this would be our last ritual as we were to be married soon and would be virgins no longer. This is as it should be. We were to become pillars of society, exemplary in every way. We were to be as Artemis is: pure of heart, quick of mind and ever watchful.

The altar was sprinkled with water from the sacred spring. Our flawless white ox was led up to the altar. She went willingly, which was a good omen. Barley was sprinkled on the ground near the great animal. After looking about at the gathered crowd, she pawed the ground once and snorted before lowering her head to eat it.

As she did, a strong priest brought out a heavy blunted hammer, raised it over his head and thumped her hard on the forehead. It seemed a brutal act, yet much less so than a butcher's shop. As her legs buckled forward and she lay stunned, another priest raised her muzzle heavenward and cut her throat with a sharp curved dagger. I turned away for a moment and thanked the ox for her sacrifice.

As the blood flowed onto the altar, we knew Artemis kept attendance as the animal's suffering was mercifully short. She approved. She would see us, we thirteen maidens representative of others our age in the country, and help us on our life journey, with our new beginning.

The ox died in sacrifice to the Goddess, so she could help us, as was a most honorable act possible for any animal. We knelt and were anointed with sacred oil on our foreheads. We arose and went forward and were marked with sacrificial blood as it was smeared upon our bare upper arms.

At the touch of the sacrificial blood, there was a sudden feeling... the descension of a high that no drink or drug could induce – yet it was drunkenness with clarity. My sight blurred slightly and my heart pulsed a bit more quickly. I closed my eyes and inhaled deeply noting the saltiness of the ocean air and din of waves crashing at the base of the cliff nearby. Our own river flowed into it; in my mind's eye, I could see the shimmer of the mixing of the fresh and salt water far below.

My senses were heightened. I smelled the burning fat, our smoke offering that caught on the wind making its way heavenward. I know not how long I remained in this state, perhaps only a few moments, yet when I returned I was thankful for the many gifts surrounding me. As I woke from this momentary glimpse of heaven, I became acutely focused on Artemis once again.

The Protectress of Children had chosen to bestow upon me many gifts and I did my best to use them for the good of all of those around me. I knew she would not leave me even as I left her temple. I loved her and could not imagine being left alone. I often spoke to her and felt her call to me in the quiet hours. Hers could be a soft presence like the glow of a candle at night or overwhelming and inescapable like a ship caught in a storm at sea. I felt renewed and more dedicated than ever to Artemis though I knew I was soon to finalize my official servitude to her.

I walked down the warm stone steps of the altar. The public ceremony was complete. As we waited for the ox to be butchered, we were able to walk among the crowd; given wide berth as we were pure and would entertain the Goddess soon. The time for feasting would come later. The fires were now being lit and meats were being spitted for roasting. The open dining rooms were being filled with flowers and finery. We did nothing except watch and enjoy. We were the honored ones.

{Melissa would alternate her personal story with that of a general cultural or background line of the story. Sometimes I would watch the actual conversational exchange – as if I could see inside her memories. I have included such a conversational exchange below.}

I sought a quiet place to rest before the private ceremony. A stone bench beckoned me from under a weatherworn tree overlooking the ocean. As I approached, I saw the white flower I had dropped earlier in the day. The slightest of smiles pulled at the corners of my mouth. I picked it up and cradled it in my lap as I sat down facing the festivities. He would be close, perhaps watching me even now.

"A she-bear was once given to this sanctuary of Artemis and was tamed," a deep voice said behind me. It was a voice reflective of an older man, someone who had seen much. I was startled, as it came from the far side of the tree, but felt intrigued as well.

"I know this story well," I said without turning around. "A young temple girl was playing with the bear, and the bear accidentally blinded her. The girl's brother, in grief for her, killed the bear."

"And a great famine befell all Athenians, far and wide because Artemis was angry at them for the killing of the bear," he continued.

"You are a wonderful storyteller," I said, not looking in his direction, "and so please tell me how the story ends."

"As punishment, in order to appease the Goddess' anger, Athenian girls, before marriage, must 'play the bear' for Artemis in ritual dance," he finished with all seriousness.

I stood and turned to face the ocean. No one knew that this man lingered so near to me. "So here we are, and I am the bear. Tell me, what part do you play?" I asked.

"I would be the cave you dwelled within, your safe haven from the baying hounds," he answered without hesitation.

He was educated. He was respectful. I hid a secret smile.

"So you wish to tame me?"

"Ah, but I know that I could not tame you any more than I could tame fire…and why would I want to…fire is beautiful, even when it is destructive," he replied.

I'm sure he was smiling, though I could not see his face. He wanted me, yet he was not crude; quite the opposite. I felt complimented as my cheeks burned hotly. I felt the honesty of his words. They sank deep within me and my heart quickened. I loved him in that moment, for he was my match, and I know my eyes betrayed me.

I laid the white flower gently on the bench. I could say no further words. I was so happy and so sad at the same time. I walked away from him and toward the crowd of people celebrating and offering their own gifts to the Goddess. He followed and said only one word so softly that only I could hear; 'please'.

Without turning around I said almost as low and much more quickly, "I am promised in marriage. Though my heart knows you, I am an honorable and noble woman of Athens; a true servant to the Goddess Artemis. There can be nothing more."

I left him standing alone in a sea of people.

{I know she was greatly saddened to leave him, yet there was such a feeling of self-respect and respect for her family and her Goddess that to do anything else would have been unthinkable and completely selfish.}

As the full moon rose into the sky, we young women shed our robes and danced in the inner courtyard for the Goddess and for no one else. As the flute played, we moved with the fire shadows of the night. I became the bear and honored her life and death. Playful and sweet, ferocious and wild and finally slow and lumbering, the music swayed the mood as the hours drew on into early morning. As the last of the twinkling stars went to sleep, a rosy hue painted the sky. We retired, our dance completed at last.

The Great She-Bear should be pleased. We walked down narrow steps into her cavern temple, escorted to the most sacred inner sanctum deep underground. We rested on soft animal skins as exhaustion took over. We were given water to drink from the sacred spring. Smoke snaked upwards from the rare incense burned on this holy occasion. This was the closest we would ever come to our virgin Goddess.

Drums beat a slow rhythm outside, yet we could hear it, muted. It was very warm and comfortable here. I watched steam rising steadily from an open chasm in the floor…a gift from our Goddess… the breathing of this gift bestowing visions and prophecy. It somehow made me feel unencumbered; freed from my body and mind in a way that I cannot explain.

I saw spirits from many times passing by in this realm; many were wandering, but others were aware and acknowledged my presence. One stepped forward, a lady, and I knew her to be one of my ancestors. She spoke to me. She said that my family were very pleased and would watch over me. I was satisfied when she finally departed and resting quietly when I heard Artemis speak to me.

"You have pleased me. Do not fear for I will never leave you. You are my special daughter and I wish you to be happy. I am content that you have found your match in love and yet you know your duties. You have honored yourself; you have respected your family and the man to whom you are promised. Though you have not spoken the words, I have heard the plea in your heart. When I give you what you most desire, will you, when I ask it of you, return to me and give me what I most desire?"

"Yes," I replied, for who can deny a Goddess.

{There was a gap in the story at this point because I think it was a difficult transition into her new home life. Her patience was definitely tested.}

I waited for my husband-to-be at my father's house for four long years. Many of my friends had married and started families already. I was secretly envious, for I only knew that my betrothed had been married already and lost his wife and child in the birthing. I could only assume that he mourned them still...and so I waited.

I was patient, and, of course there are always opportunities for a woman to be satisfied by a man, but I declined all advances and would-be suitors. I filled my time caring for my brothers and sisters, sewing, gardening and reading books to all children of both slaves and the estate alike. It was a satisfying life. Naturally, I never stopped my servitude to Artemis. I worshipped her in my very attitude of living; I helped those people whose lives I touched when they required it. They did not have to ask.

At times, people of many walks of life would bring wounded or motherless animals to my father's house so that I could care for them. It was my greatest service to the Goddess and it became well known that our house was friendly refuge for all sorts of wild animals. I was the caretaker; though we released many that were brought to us back into the wild.

{Melissa was known as a very gifted and kind young woman. Her family was well-known and respected, yet she was respected in her own right.}

One day, not long after I grew into my nineteenth year, a stranger rode through our gate. I watched as he dismounted and handed the reins of his fine horse to our stable boy. He carefully lifted a small package lying across his mount's saddle and handed it to another servant – giving him some specific instruction. A third servant of our house offered the man water to wash his hands and wine to slake his thirst. He accepted and asked for the master of the house; my father.

My father went out to meet him. He was offered the customary traveler's courtesy of a place to sleep and something to eat. I did not see this stranger again until after dinner when I was summoned to the courtyard.

The stranger, now bathed and cleanly-dressed, was standing near the fountain with his back turned to me. The sky was draped in golden hues as shadows began their slow walk across the courtyard, content for their moment in the sun.

"Welcome to our home," I said as I entered the garden. He turned at the sound of my voice.

"Thank you. I am very comfortable here," he said.

I nodded and sat down on a bench near some blooming orange flowers. I was quiet. Quietude is comfortable. It isn't necessary to fill empty space with words. This seemed to unnerve the stranger somewhat.

"Aren't you curious as to who I am or why I am here," he asked.

"The fact that my father has invited you to stay as a guest in our home means that you are welcome. I do not question why. I am content that you are here and will wait patiently until you see fit to tell me what you like."

He smiled. I must have amused him.

"I confess I came here because of you. The local people know you as a gifted healer of animals. I was hunting in a wood not far from here and shot a fine-looking doe. It is not the season for foaling, so I was surprised when I discovered a fawn hiding in the brush. I have brought her here as penance to Artemis. Your father tells me you serve the Goddess well. Tell me, will you raise her and release her on my behalf?"

I had not noticed the spotted fawn sleeping in the shadows at his feet.

"I would be honored."

"No, it is I who am honored by you. Come to me, my Melissa, for I am Lysander of Sparta, your betrothed. I have been away fighting the Persians in service to Pausanias and the Allies. I am a man of standing in the cavalry. I will provide you a good life, with love, if you will allow it."

I don't know how I could have missed it before, but there was the tell-tale sign tied around the fawn's neck…a white flower…just the same as I had dropped those many years before.

The man, Lysander, had aged since I had seen him last, his skin so dark that he looked foreign to me. His clothes were not usual and he had grown a beard…yet when I looked into his eyes, I recognized my heart's desire. Before I knew it the distance between us was crossed and I had fallen into his arms.

"I knew your heart would stay true to mine," he whispered, "I knew it the day I saw you walking to Brauron. I knew it the moment you said you were betrothed and walked away from me; you did not know that you were to marry me. I am so sorry I could not tell you. I was to leave on campaign the very next day and have been there every day since. How would that have been if I did not return for you?"

I could say nothing. Everything had suddenly become very clear. I was thankful.

{This part of the story was very emotional for Melissa – like the best thing that could ever have happened to her, did!}

We were happy. We spent so much of our time together that our friends and family were concerned that we were too focused on having children. I assure you we were very much focused on one another. We considered that any children would be blessings. We did not discuss his previous life as I am sure it pained him to think about. We cannot control what happens in life. We do not need to discuss everything. Some thoughts and feelings are meant for us alone. Sometimes, we cannot know what another person feels; we can only offer ourselves honestly and be present now.

I dedicated the fawn to Artemis and named her Dido. She grew up to be a beautiful doe. We released her, yet she never wandered very far. Her presence reminded me that Artemis was always close, though not always in sight; that though she seemed docile, it was in her nature to be wild.

{It took a long time for the next part of the story to be conveyed to me. Melissa's energy was usually strong and I could understand her easily, yet, the emotions distorted this usual energy and dissipated our connection at times.}

As the hunter pursues the game, the chase takes many turns.

Lysander was a soldier first and foremost. His call to duty was every day. A Spartan man had his loyalties to protect and honor the city and his family. It was not a commitment that was taken lightly. It coursed through their very veins. I was with child when they brought his body back to me on his shield. Thieves had murdered a local farmer, raped his wife and daughter and stolen a flock of sheep. My husband died protecting a fellow soldier. It was an honorable death.

Words cannot convey how I felt. I cut my hair. I tore my clothes and covered myself in ashes. I wanted to die. But, the baby inside me that grew stronger with each passing day kicked so hard in her fight for life that I too began to hope for life. Yet, I knew the truth. I knew that my father desired that I be married again – and as quickly as possible so my baby would have a father. I did not want this. It would be a complete betrayal.

As I lay in our marriage bed late one night and listened to the soft falling rain, I heard Artemis speak to me for a second time.

"Return to me, my daughter, for you live in the world of men now and my greatest desire is that you should live with me. We shall raise your daughter together."

I returned to the Temple at Brauron the very next day. They had been expecting me and we were welcomed with open arms. My return had been foretold. Our baby was born a few weeks later; I named her Artemisia Lysandra.

I remained married to Lysander in my heart and never forgot my time with him. All too often I sat in the garden remembering him, his scent, his touch, the way his eyes crinkled when he smiled. The priestess' of the temple gave me great latitude in the duties I undertook. I was favored of Artemis and it showed in the sanctity of the ceremonies I performed in her honor. I entered into a deeply spiritual time in my life. It was quiet. No need to fill the space with useless words.

In time, I began to split my duties between the Acropolis and Brauron Temples. Sometimes I trained the young women, but in the later years I became the public face for the temples. We enjoyed a time of expansion and wealth. Lysandra grew up fine and strong and beautiful. She never left the temple and remained true to Artemis her entire life. She did not want to marry and so I did not ask her to marry. We must all choose our own paths or Chaos will choose for us. The measure of a woman is not how many children she can bear or how well she manages the household, but how she handles whatever life puts before her...how well she adapts.

I was not born Spartan, I am Athenian. The cultures hold some disdain for each other, yet we can learn from both. My daughter became the best that Athens and Sparta embodied; refinement, directness and loyalty to a fault. She was a source of great happiness for me. She became a High Priestess to Artemis in my twilight years. I am glad I was able to witness the event. My health was failing at this time, yet I had lived a long life.

When I lay in my bed, and I knew the end was near, I was not afraid. I was comforted by those around me. I took great comfort in my daughter – even just looking at her face I could see Lysander beckoning. Soon there would be a great homecoming and then we would wait patiently for Lysandra.

I had already said goodbye to my daughter in peace, but she remained greatly distressed until peace came to her from a presence she could not see. As my sight grew dim, I saw Dido in the room. She was a calming spirit. She had passed long ago. I reached out to pet her and she accepted my touch.

Not long after, the Goddess herself entered the room, bringing the fresh air of sunshine and the outdoors. She grasped my hand and pulled me from my body with the swiftness of an arrow shot from her bow. I felt no pain. The Goddess smiled warmly; she spoke no words yet I knew that Lysander waited for me in the Elysian Fields. I hastened to him accompanied by the Lovely Huntress, Artemis of the Animals Wild and my sweet Dido.

Ahmaret

750 AD in Damascus (Syria)

It took a long time to fall asleep on the night of July 27, 2009, but when I did, I can remember my dream very well. I stood in the middle of what seemed to be a place of nothingness; grey space with no floor, ceiling or walls. I was waiting to go somewhere.

As I waited, I began to feel a sort of humming sensation under my feet. Surprisingly, when I looked down, I was standing on a disc of blue light, flying high over the world. I traveled but for a moment when the disc began to descend through the clouds and over a dry, barren land.

It was hot and bright as the disc stopped and hovered right over the ground. I stepped off of the cool disc and onto burning sand. The sun was scorching overhead as the blue disc dissipated into nothing. I feel I have arrived in an ancient time in an early culture. For now, I am alone and in the middle of nowhere.

After a moment, my eyes began to adjust to the bright desert sun. Heat waves rose up in the distance from the hills of sand. As my eyes searched the horizon, I found the long black line of a caravan snaking from the distance. I stood directly in its path.

I then heard a young woman's voice; "It is a luxury to be able to make choices for yourself; it was not always this way," she said. "To be wasteful with your decisions is to be ungracious for the opportunity you have been given."

The camels were coming closer and I could see the merchants, goods and various people that were walking alongside. At this point, I noticed a young girl dressed all in black, her face covered with a long scarf, revealing only her eyes. She carried a younger boy; most likely not her son, but rather a brother.

What follows is their story as she wished it to be told. Both of these souls are reborn again and walk the Earth today, and though they are much changed, their essence is still very much the same.

Use Your Mind

My name is Ahmaret. I am a princess of the rural lands two moons walk from the great City of Damascus and farther still from the blue of the Mediterranean Sea. My father was a proud ruler and had taken many wives in marriage. I was blessed because my mother was his favorite wife. She was also his first wife. She gave him only me and my brother as heirs, yet, we were held favorite above all others.

My brother was the prince and heir to our father's lands and I was to be a first wife to the ruler of the province next to ours, as a sign of peace and allegiance. Sadly, this was not to be.

My father loved horses. It was his hobby, though truly it was a great weakness for him. Our family owned a great herd of horses and some were greatly prized over others. He named his favorites, raced them and bred them for swiftness and beauty.

One day, a trader came to our lands with a wildly beautiful black stallion. We had never seen it's equal. My father offered the trader many gold pieces in order to buy the horse, however; the trader replied that the horse was not for sale. Indeed, it had been promised to another.

Many offers were made, but all were politely refused. My father never accepted 'no' for an answer when it came to a horse that he wanted. He arranged for the prize to be stolen, hidden and secretly added to our stock. The plan was carried out, but the trader was not fooled.

No one knew that the trader was our neighboring province's young prince to whom I was promised in marriage. Nor did we know that the horse was to be gifted to me as a wedding present. It had been a test of integrity for our people, for the leadership always reflects the disposition of the people.

We had enjoyed much prosperity, perhaps to the point of being spoiled and indifferent instead of gracious and kind. When we received message that my long promised marriage was cancelled and the reasons why, my father was outraged and insulted. He sent that beautiful black horse to the prince in pieces the following day. I was sickened, yet it was not my place to speak.

The attack happened suddenly. No one expected it. I do not wish to dwell upon this, for it was a terrible sight. The palace, my home, was in flames and my family and servants were being killed in front of my eyes. An elderly nursemaid came to me and handed over my 4-year old brother.

I saw my father for but a moment, but he looked straight into my eyes and made me promise to maintain my purity and station in life and to marry only as a first wife and someone befitting of a princess of his royal blood. He wanted strong grandsons to carry on his line. I promised.

I was to care for my brother and raise him as my father wished, lacking nothing and given privileges. How this was to happen I was not sure; but I made this promise as well. The rest of this memory is a blur.

We were covered in dark servant's clothes, given a small sack of hard bread and salted meat. Necklaces of gold were placed around my neck. We were smuggled out through a secret tunnel; only the two of us with our familiar nursemaid Rana so we would not attract undue attention.

As we continued into the darkness and void of the desert, Rana told us not to turn around and to never come back. She did not come with us. I have always wondered what happened to her.

I covered my brother's face from the wind and sand and turned for a moment; our city was burning. I became aware of the tears wet on my cheeks. My brother, though he was confused, did not cry. He was quiet as he watched; I could see the flames of the distant fire reflected in his brown eyes. All I knew was now gone; my family, my privilege, my everything.

We turned away from the city and started walking with the others… walking into darkness. The darkness became a place for my mind to re-member that which had just happened. It had been surreal. I saw my moth-er, with her fine bones and large almond shaped eyes, lying on a richly embroidered couch near her favorite lotus pool. She looked as if she were peacefully at sleep, though her caramel rich coloring had paled. Her arm had fallen to the side and off of the couch.

It was then that I saw the dark red blood pooled on the floor below. There was so much blood and still flowing from her lovely wrist. It was the pool of blood, that moment that I saw the flash of the wound and the blood dripping from her fingers, and my abhorrence of the scene that kept playing and replaying. It was as if every time that memory played, I relived that moment of horror anew.

I had already said a tearful goodbye to her. I understood why she did it; she would not be shamed. She said she was a proud and proper wife and that I could learn by her example in all things; that I should remember her in my everyday life by making the proper choices. I would honor her in this manner.

She would not be taken by the enemy in any way. She would not dishonor her marriage and cause my father embarrassment. She would be remembered well by our family. Her final words came back to me throughout my entire life; always turn your face to the sun and the shadows will fall behind you.

It would soon be morning and the sun would rise to greet us. I heard others crying and comforting one another. There was no one to comfort me. My mother had loved us, though it was not required. She had shown us kindness and gentleness. I am glad to know that she did not suffer. I imagined that her soul looked down upon us from the great starry sky above and I was calmed.

{We paused for a moment, taking time for respect. We moved forward in time.}

I had never been away from our city. I was 15 years old. As I was a young woman, I had never gone anywhere without an escort, so I was afraid. The gold that I wore was very heavy and my brother, Damar, did not want to walk. So I walked and I carried him and I wore the gold and was exhausted.

Our people believe that eyes tell the story of your soul; indeed, many a man will marry or not marry a woman having seen only her eyes, thinking they can know her by this alone. I felt that, if anyone should have looked into my eyes at that time, they would have known only great sadness and fear; so I looked away from others.

I wished no one to know me or to help me, for I was proud, and I did not accept that we were now orphans requiring pity. I could not say what our futures would hold. We were alone in the great wide world, and no one would care for us, and I was held by such great promises.

{The walking went on for two days time. I heard much complaining from her about the heat, cold and sand. At midday on day one, their group happened upon a resting caravan of merchants and travelers. There were many refugees from her village that were also making their way to the large city of Damascus. The two groups

joined for increased safety. Food and drink were available, as was a sleeping place for them.}

On the morning of the third day, we saw a great monstrous wall rising up before us. It seemed to enclose the entire city. I could see the wood and mud brick buildings that lay within; great huge buildings of a height that I'd never seen before. It hummed with activity and seemed quite wonderfully chaotic until the stench stopped us in our tracks.

Damar buried his face in my shoulder. It became worse the closer we walked toward the gate. Waste littered the ground. Herds of goats, sheep and asses crowded and competed for space as we made our way through the gate entrance. I saw beggars and cripples lining the walls, asking the passersby for money and food. Sick people had covered themselves with fabric, yet I could see that they were missing limbs and eyes and even their noses to the illness which afflicted them.

I passed all of these quickly and without instance, yet I paused when I saw a young girl who looked much like me. I sent Damar over to her with a small gold coin. It was a lot of money for her...and then I realized it was a lot of money for us. I prayed that God would bless and keep her safe and healthy. I prayed the same for us.

The caravan disbanded and we were left to ourselves. We began our search for a place to stay where questions would not be asked. I found such a place in a hard part of the city, an unforgiving place where fornication for money was commonplace. I was shocked, but I had heard stories of such places.

I lied to the hotelier, saying that we were meeting my husband the next day. I was very pleased with myself, having secured a room, some food and a bath for Damar and me. We ate, drank and bathed ourselves and then fell asleep without delay.

It had been a mistake. I had made a huge mistake. I was not a practiced liar. When I awoke, every piece of gold we owned was gone. I had not hidden it well enough. My heart sank to my stomach and I cried until there were no more tears. I had only paid for one night. I had planned on moving around until I could figure out what to do.

I was sure the hotelier had stolen my gold; he was a very smug man thereafter. It was not a secret that he desired me. Now, without any way to pay, he thought I might satisfy his desires for our room and supper. He knew I was not a married woman. He knew we were alone. He was wrong, though, for I would not bend to anyone's will save that of my father or future husband. We slept outside the next night, and it was very cold, but I slept clean and without sin. I thought of my mother; what would she do? Face to the sun; find work.

The next day, we walked around the area and I played games with Damar. We pretended to be part of a family that had just moved to the area. A kind baker two doors away from the hotel gave us some sweet bread in a gesture of welcome, surely hoping we would bring him business. We certainly spoke like genteel people.

As Damar and I walked along the streets, we pretended to visit the shops, but after a few weeks, given our deteriorating appearance, we were found out easily and shooed away. I tried to lie, but to no avail. We were obviously without escort and homeless.

There was a fountain in the district where many people gathered. This place drew people together. A market of sorts would pop up on certain days; moreover, it seemed that men would trade or make bargains with one another here. Unfortunately, though there were upstanding men making trades, they could not be bothered with us; moreover, there were also men of low character.

After many weeks, a few men quietly approached me, having seen only my eyes, and asked for some time with me. I was outraged. How dare they! My answer was always the same, always an emphatic no. One particularly disgusting man smiled and said he would see me the next week and the week after that until the little boy was hungry enough for me to consider his request. He said the longer I waited, the worse it would be for me. I gathered Damar to me and I told the man that if he knew who I was, he would not dare speak to me in such a way. I told him he was a dead man walking if I told my father. Lying was a forgivable sin. No matter what happened, I would never dishonor myself or my family with such an act of shame.

Even worse, I am ashamed that more than once did a man approach me with offers of money if they could have some time with my brother. I was repulsed. We were not born to do such things. It is a disgrace and against God to think such a thing. I told them that they should feel shame for their asking.

I learned that it was good to be known as chaste. I stopped lying, but I did not tell our true story to anyone. I stopped using servant's words and acted the simpleton no longer. I was not above work and indeed, sought it out daily in the market. No family of respect would hire me, though I was a fine weaver. No one knew anything about me and I was a young lady without an escort and with a child...which meant I had no respect and was shunned by most everyone.

More than a month passed and with each passing day I became thinner and weaker. Damar fared better, as charity for children was smiled upon, but we were dirty and smelled terrible. My skin became dry and rough; the weather was not our friend. I dreamt of the rich baths and oils my skin once knew. It seemed that our previous life had been a dream.

I tried to occupy Damar with songs and stories, but he wanted to know why we couldn't have our own rooms and good food like before. He was only four, yet, he had been given every luxury. He did not ask about mother and father, I think he remembered enough.

For now, we only had one another, and life on the streets was hard. My plan was to continue to search for a place to weave and I would work. Our lives were in God's hands, but it would be up to us to take action. This seemed a test of my integrity; but I would grow stronger from it and not relent what I knew to be right.

Then, as it happened, in a single chance meeting, our lives changed forever. One person is all that it takes to change the world. One person following what they know to be right can change so much with a single right decision. Maybe they will not leave monuments, but they change the world on a much deeper level; they contribute kindness and love to a world that needs it. This is how you make a true mark in the world; this is how you are remembered.

On a typical dry and sunny afternoon, a man I had not seen before came to the fountain. I noticed him as he noticed me. It was a moment separate from the time and space in which we lived. His eyes were very kind. He did not regard me with pity as did so many others. He sent his servant to me with some bread and wine. I sent it back to him. He sent it a second time, and the servant said thus, that the bread was for the child and nothing was expected in return. I broke the loaf in half, kept half and sent half back with the servant. An understanding was made; I would not accept charity from him for myself. I would owe him nothing.

The man sent his servant every day for two weeks. He never asked for anything and always sent food. I gave it all to Damar. He became much happier as his stomach stopped aching with hunger. He looked forward to seeing the kind old servant appear. With Damar's new health came my physical demise for I had not eaten for so long. I think the servant must have spoken with his master and gave him the news for a woman servant came alone the next day and offered to take us to her master's home so we could bathe and eat a proper meal.

Nothing is free, so I asked what payment was to be expected. The servant replied that the master had heard that I was a weaver and he had need of my services. A rug of high quality would be expected in payment. I agreed to these terms and was elated, though I felt guarded, even with this strange man's kindness.

I asked the servant many questions. She did not answer them, stating that her master would be the proper person from whom to request information. His servants were loyal; it was a good sign. I knew not why this man was helping us, yet I was grateful for the opportunity to pay our way. I may have come from great wealth and royal blood, but I knew the satisfaction of work well done. God had decided that I was to work, and so, I would work and be grateful for the opportunity.

The servant told me that her master's name was Serra. We walked about an hour until we were in a nice part of the city. It felt comfortable and safe. The odiferous smell of the city was noticeably absent. His house was large and very clean, yet modest and respectful in its decoration.

Serra had two servants; a man and a woman both of great age. It was apparent that they cared for him; in their service they showed much respect and love. They had been with him for a long time, and they say that he cares for them and makes sure that their needs are more than provided.

The first order of business was to get clean. I was bathed in deliciously hot water drawn by his woman servant and for the first time in over two months, my skin knew the richness of expensive oil. My clothes were burned and new ones given over to me, scented with perfume. I almost felt as if I were back home again…except that I was gaunt now, hardly a shadow of my former self.

Damar was clean and happy when I saw him, eating white grapes and honeyed cakes in the courtyard. The master of the home did not return for many weeks. He was visiting with his first wife and her parents as well as conducting some business in that region. Meanwhile, Damar and I became re-accustomed to fine living. Truly, I had not forgotten our terms and so had asked for a loom and threads so that I could begin my weaving.

When Serra returned, I was treated with much respect; always there was someone accompanying me when he and I were together. It was a marker of respect. Men are never allowed to be alone with women of respect until they are married to one another.

Time passes quickly when one is satisfied. Three years went by in the blink of an eye. I often watched as Serra played with Damar in the courtyard. He was treated with much kindness. I often wondered about Serra's past.

The woman servant, Shreva, eventually told me that Serra's first wife chose not to live with him. He had allowed her choice and she had moved back to her parent's home. She had given him sons and daughters and raised them well, but there had been no love between man and wife. It had been an arranged marriage, so she had performed her wifely duties and obeyed his wishes and that was all. His second and third wives were dead; one in childbirth and the other from sickness.

I never asked Serra about his past; his personal feelings were not for me to know unless he chose to tell me. I knew he would marry me if I encouraged him, but I could not be anything if not a first wife...and so it was impossible. I did not encourage his interest, yet I was not cold to him. It was clear, however, that he respected my decision.

In time, as it takes much time to weave a rug of quality, Damar asked me if Serra could be his father. I encouraged his acceptance of Serra in this role and also made it known to Serra of my wishes. This seemed to make them both happy.

Serra was not strict and gave over anything that made Damar happy. Yet, Serra was a good man with morals and values closely aligned with my own. He was a wealthy merchant not given over to sin. I accepted this arrangement for my brother as it was for the best. Serra's children were grown and married and had children of their own. My promise to my father with concerns to my brother was now fulfilled.

I enjoyed Serra's company and so we spent many hours in the garden and talked about a great many things, and in time, I came to love him. This was very unconventional, but, I was an exception to many rules. I was allowed a personality with him, to have my own opinion, and he did not expect my obedience. He delighted in my thoughts and ideas. I found him to have a good sense of humor. We were an odd pair; two pieces of a puzzle perfectly fitted.

Yet, I was bound by a promise and I could not relent. There was to be no fulfillment for me even as I partially fulfilled my promise to my father. Alas, I would give him no grandsons. I made the choice that if I could not be with Serra, then I would be with no one. I dared not betray my heart. I had comfort, security and companionship.

Serra never asked about my past, though in time, I told him everything. I was ashamed that I lived when I knew that my family surely did not. If they had survived, they would have come looking for me.

Since I could not marry Serra and keep my promise to my father, we avoided temptation and made arrangements to move my rooms to separate quarters within his estate.

I spent much time with Serra and I feel that we were more than the best of friends. I kept myself covered as was proper. He had only seen my eyes, but, I know that he could see the love I held for him and it was enough. I could feel the love he held for me. We needed not consummate our love to know that it was real. Life was good to us, even if we could not completely fulfill our complete desires.

On Damar's sixteenth birthday, Serra gave him a horse. It was a beautiful black stallion with a lively spirit. It reminded me of a time long ago, however, in some way it was Serra's way to help me make peace with the past. Damar was so pleased; his enthusiasm for horses matched my father's. However, being raised by Serra, Damar had become much different than my father. Not only could he read, write and work numbers, he could use knowledge and reason out good solutions. He placed high value on respect and morals. I was so proud of him. Yet, for certain, Damar loved to have fun and the pair of them (Damar and his horse) caused much mischief in our household and with his friends.

{These were happy times that were remembered fondly. Of course, I think there was much more sadness that surrounded her relationship with Serra, that they could never be together, and yet there was always a feeling of thankfulness. He had taken care of them and yet allowed her to know that she added value to his life and his home.}

I finished the rug for Serra's home. I had spent many long years weaving it. I had not known what pattern I would use when I started it. I had simply started weaving. The pattern that developed became a reflection of hardships suffered and incorporated what seemed to me a long journey and finally the colorful treads of hope and love. It was very unusual, yet, by all accounts it was a work of art and beautiful to behold. He honored me by placing it on the wall at the entrance to his home. Many guests made comments at its luxurious oddity. It reflected my personality and my life journey in many ways. It was reflective of our beautifully odd relationship.

One day, not long after I finished the rug and my payment for our way of living, I went to visit with my Serra. I was told that he was not yet awake, which was very unusual. I asked the servants join me and we visited his bedchamber on a Sunday mid-afternoon. We found him seemingly asleep in his bed. It was then that I knew he had passed from the realm of the living and into that of the dead. My heart broke that day and has still not mended.

With so much loss in that life, it was hard for me to continue. Though I did think of Serra every day, I was able to find the sweetness in each day that I knew he would savor. A wayward seed that would grow into a beautiful flower in a peculiar place, hot tea on a cool morning, the utter joy in a baby's laugh…I would smile to myself and appreciate the moment.

As Serra's belongings were divided amongst his heirs, my brother was treated as one of his sons. The rug became my possession through him. Even though it reflected many aspects of my life, it no longer reflected who I was at that time. You see, we change as we go through life…our experiences, the people we meet…it changes us. One day, if we are lucky, we are able to look back and think about that strange person that we once were. For me, it was as if I had lived several lives within the span of my years. Death, for me, was a kind rest. When I closed my eyes for the final time, I was so happy, because I knew when I opened them again, I would see my Serra.

Perhaps if I had but taken a moment to think for myself, my life would have taken a different path. I should have realized that my father was gone and that he held nothing over me. Still, at that time, the memory and authority of my father and men in general, kept me from happiness, kept control over me even after his death. Serra and I could have married and had many children and would have been very happy.

Nothing past remains. Nothing future is certain. No one should control how you feel; you must make your own decisions. Otherwise, you are living your life according to someone else's rules.

I want to tell you that in the year of 2010, I have found my soul mate once again on this earthly plane. It seems that we are presented opportunities over and again until we learn what we need to learn. Somehow, these many years later, the choice was before me once again. I could have chosen to stay in an unhappy marriage as religion and my father dictated on pain of punishment in hell or leave that terrible situation and follow my heart to happiness. I chose happiness.

I did take some time to sort out my feelings. I now know and realize that what I think and feel has worth. I left my husband and a loveless marriage; I released him to find his own happiness. It was not easy, but it was necessary, even if he did not think so at the time. In this year of 2011, he is now happily married to someone else.

I can truly say that it is never too late to find your voice and follow your heart to happiness.

2

Angels, Guides And Those Who Watch Over Us

We Are Not Alone

I was five years old when I saw an angel for the first time. He was standing high in the branches of a tree, shining in a beautiful light. My mother, father, younger sister and I had been traveling far from home in the State of West Virginia on vacation. A car had been weaving on both sides of the narrow road on which we were driving as it came towards us. I don't really remember the accident, only seeing the front of our truck crumble like aluminum foil as the impact happened.

We had just been in a terrible 60 mph head-on collision and yet there were no serious injuries. No one in either vehicle had been wearing seat-belts. As we were in the middle of nowhere in the mountains, it took 45 minutes for the ambulance to arrive. For me, it seemed instantaneous. I lost that time somehow. I just know that when I opened my eyes, my angel was there watching over me and I wasn't even a bit surprised.

This many years later, I think about the innocence of a child's perspective. It's fairly simple, they don't question what they see and they see many things that adults dismiss as childish musings. I see wisdom in their honest words and hope to recapture some of that innocence myself.

I know I have been searching for my purpose for all of my life in some aspect, yet, hadn't really recognized what I was doing. I have made many mistakes, won and lost difficult challenges, traveled the world and kept on searching. It has been elusive, yet I am persistent if nothing else. Understand that I had more than a few lessons to learn along the way.

It seems that achieving some balance in life is necessary in order to really recognize what we are supposed to do. As well, for some of us know-it-alls, a humbling of knowing that you really know nothing may be required; a realization that there are beings and energy out there more that we can see or know. This is not difficult, just some simple knowledge that we can learn from any child.

I have been aware of a presence close to me since I was very small. I had no name for it, no explanation, yet I never felt alone. We played together in my back yard and she became my invisible friend. I told no one about her. She taught me how to read in one afternoon. We made May Day flower baskets together with violets and dandelions. She is one reason that my childhood was not lonely.

When I grew old enough, I began to deny her existence. Religion taught that entities such as her were evil demons. My family was very religious and would never understand my relationship with her. It was too much to think of her as evil, so it was easier to believe that she only existed in my mind; that I had made her up.

In my teen years, I denied God's very existence; a pendulum will swing both ways. I had blindly believed everything in my childhood and so I began to doubt everything in my college years. I began to think that I was doing everything on my own without any assistance. How naïve!

The point is that we can deny the existence of our angels, guides and even God, but that does not mean they stop helping us. The very thoughts we think can put them into action. I look back now at pictures of my travels and see my guide, whom I have come to know as Elisabeth, as a bright blue orb in many of the photos. I think back to some of the strangers I met on my travels and know that we did not meet by happenstance, for what I learned in our meeting changed my views extraordinarily enough that I could keep opening my mind and continue learning.

Your angels are assigned to you and will never leave you. You have but to request assistance and they will move into action. You may not always recognize their presence, especially if you are distraught in any way. Our emotions sometimes create blocks against listening or feeling. Know that they are there. You can speak to them, call to them and ask for help.

Keep in mind that asking for help does not mean that you can sit back and relax; you still have to lead the effort and diligently pursue your goal. Angels will not complete your goals for you. It is your life, after all, and your choice. At times, you may not seem to get the answers you want – this may be a blessing in disguise. Oftentimes they can see consequences and outcomes that we cannot even imagine.

It is my experience that we have many guides to help us on our life journey, yet perhaps one specific guide that works with us since our soul's inception. My guide, Elisabeth, is my constant companion. I choose to acknowledge her and accept her help and guidance. She is not a God or Goddess; she simply guides and comforts me. Her role in my life of recent is much expanded and I feel at ease with the many changes happening... indeed, my life is no longer stagnant. I'm never sure what's around the next bend. That's what happens when you embrace change, so be mindful of what you request, you may just get it!

It would seem to me now that our purpose in life may not be singular; instead it may be more of a flow or direction where that purpose will continually change and allow you to be in the most effective place you can be while continuing your learning. Also, once you think you've mastered something, expect fully to be tested on it over and over until you get it just right—and are no longer challenged when dealing with that situation.

Mr. Fennick

1900 in the Northeast Region of the United States

Mr. Fennick came to me on April 20th, 2008 during a lucid dream. He was the first visitor that I recognized as such. I would wake up in the early morning hours and feel compelled to get up and write down the dreaming I was seeing. I came to realize that it was a continuous story with the same main character. It was a story someone was telling me.

Mr. Fennick was the first because at the end of one dreaming sequence I asked him his name and could remember it. I think it surprised him just as much as it surprised me. Before long, I became very tired from too many early mornings and so I invited Mr. Fennick to tell me his story as I sat with my laptop one evening. It didn't take long and I was back to a normal sleep routine. I looked forward to sitting with him in the hour or so before bedtime.

It was difficult, though, because I felt all of his emotions. I cried many tears of sadness and desperation. He shared his feelings with me – and I feel that this was perhaps healing for him to know that I empathized with his life story. There was a true lack of understanding for him in his living life.

I promised him that I would share his story and that others would come to know and understand him as well. In some way, I think he needed to tell his story and be understood in order to move on. I believe he was already on the Other Side when he came to me, yet, I know that he was not reborn onto this earth...not since his previous lifetime. He needed this healing in order to be reborn.

This story was given to me over a course of weeks for about an hour or so at a time. It took several more weeks to refine it to the point where I was satisfied with the wording, but more importantly, Mr. Fennick was satisfied. Late one evening I read the story for a final time, and as I read the ending lines, I felt satisfaction – Mr. Fennick's satisfaction. He lingered for a moment more as I felt a warm energy touch and move within my heart. Mr. Fennick departed. I did not and have not to this day heard from Mr. Fennick again. He has gone.

He told me this story, one that he asked me to re-tell. He wanted simply to be remembered- perhaps not as the old man he had become, but as the man he once was; a strong young man his grandchildren never knew. To his kin, should they ever read this story, he sends his love. Mostly he wants them to know that he is fine and looks forward to seeing them when their time comes to cross over. He will be waiting. The following is Mr. Fennick's story in his own words.

Seasons

I was the first-born son of third generation farmers. I had eleven brothers and sisters. We all worked the land in the beginning. When I look back now, I see that those were good days. Strength of body and mind, the hot sun and the dark warm earth in our hands; there is nothing complicated in the planting of seeds. Plant them, care for them and they grow.

World War I happened and I do not want to speak of those happenings except to say that quite naively, I enlisted in 1917 when I was just 16 years old. I was not the youngest to serve my country. One of my friends was only fourteen when he died. It was a hard time. Being a simple man does not help in times of war or conflict. The heart knows what is right and what is wrong. Killing a man does not kill the ideal he fights for…that can only be changed by the way we raise our children.

The Great Depression followed in 1929 and we, as so many others, fell upon hard times. Many of my brothers and sisters left to find work in the city. Some of them I never saw again. I think this was hardest on my parents. Not only did we lose help for our farm, we lost a bit of ourselves in their leaving. A large family always makes a lot of noise – you notice when it's gone.

Somewhere along the way, sadly, my parents passed on and I buried them on a hill near a grove of apple trees on our farm. It is what they wanted. I inherited the farm and knew I would stay; I had none of the wanderlust my siblings possessed. I loved the land and the seasons. It was what I had always known.

I married my childhood sweetheart and we started a family right away. We were born for each other and knew it as soon as we met. I was 22 and she was 17. We had few precious happy years together. She died in childbirth and I did not think I would recover; I suppose in many ways, I never really did. Thank the heavens that our daughter survived to keep me from my grief.

I did not remarry, and many times felt that my wife was still with me. I spoke to her often when I was alone in the fields. I loved her so much. Death did not separate us but in the physical. There was to be no one else for me. I buried her near my parents and visited often.

When World War II happened, I did not want any part of it. I was almost too old to worry about being drafted. So many boys left hometowns never to return again. It was a sad time. Throughout wartime and the following years, I buried several of my brothers and sisters, most of whom had moved away and lived their lives. They came to me strangers in appearance, though I still remember them as they were when we were growing up. Sadly, time never stops. Enjoy the times as they happen. It is the only way to live.

The time came when my daughter passed on and "authorities" would not allow me to bury her on our farm. Her family wanted her to have a "proper" burial and a "proper" resting place. I don't know what would be more proper than to be buried with family on family land. I put a headstone for her next to her mother's. Family should be buried together. As in life, so it should be in death.

I was old when she departed – but not so old to be out of my mind. It's hard how people discount your feelings and sanity when you grow older. Perhaps it is a blessing when one begins to lose a grasp of reality. Loneliness is hell.

[*The story breaks at this point and I am left alone for awhile. When Mr. Fennick returns to finish the story, he has brought us into the "present" timeframe. He is in the middle of a visit with his grand-daughter and her fiancée.*]

They were speaking in hushed tones in the living room. I heard snippets of their conversation, and the words were unmistakable: old, senile, shouldn't be alone, something has to change. They were deciding my fate without a word to me directly.

They had come under the guise of a wedding invitation. My granddaughter and her slick fiancée sat rather uncomfortably on my comfortable old couch. City folk. It was a sad end to my family in my opinion. Yet each of us has the right to choose and that is the important factor, I suppose. In retrospect, it's really what we Americans fought those wars for...freedom in its many aspects.

I stood in the kitchen making coffee for my unexpected guests. This was my house. I built it and knew every line of it. A flood of sunshine tumbled through the open window over the sink. Open windows allowed in a sweet smelling breeze, but also dust and all manner of bugs – much to my wife's dismay. God rest her soul. I'll be with her soon.

A few brown chickens clucked outside the window, scratching through the dust and finding a tasty morsel every now and then. A wedding was news, and of course I should be there; yet the possibility of not returning to my home was unacceptable. How could I leave this place that comforted me so? I had lived here for over 75 years.

When did I become such a burden to my family? How could I have known how to plan for a century of living on this earth? How could I have calculated that I would outlive all that I held dear and loved without restraint? I know I shouldn't get so worked up; but change for the sake of change is ridiculous. I am fine right where I am; change at this point in my life is simply too much to ask.

The percolating coffee smelled good; nice familiar sound. It was bitter and strong; the very taste of the color black. As I looked at the hands resting on the sink, I did not, at first, think they were mine. Age spots and wiry, white hair curled on crooked knuckles...yes, they were mine. How cruel that life sharpens the mind with experience as age advances and the body slowly fails itself. My hands reminded me of an old oak tree in my yard; scarred and twisted from the trials of the winter and wind...but knowing of the anchor of the earth. I know the feel of warm dark dirt, and cold stark soil; it gives life and accepts death and it is my friend and confidant.

My farm is 140 acres and at one time I farmed it all. Now, it sits fallow resting. Rather like I do. The woodlands have reclaimed some and random crops of corn and alfalfa still grow lackadaisically. I don't wander my entire property anymore, though I do catch the occasional trespassers, usually young boys smoking in the old farmhouse. I won't sell it. Ever. Not a single acre. This land has been good to me.

There is so much that the younger generation does not understand. Hard to communicate with them most of the time. I'm not sure that they want to listen so much as they want to be heard. I accepted my granddaughter's invitation and watched as they held my heavy white coffee mugs so awkwardly in their hands.

Sunshine streamed through the window and into the living room in bright rays illuminating those tiny specks of dust floating through the air as the steam rose from their coffee through it all. It was a timeless, clarifying moment. It is as if I suddenly knew something that had escaped me all my years and then just as quickly, it was gone. Like a spell broken. Yet, I felt better about the visit.

They had seemed pleased. They drove away down the gravel road, brushing by the wildflowers without notice. The old fence falling down in disrepair, supported only by the tall grass and occasional tree, ran beside their fancy red car until they drove out of sight. I could only imagine the city man who had just visited cursing about the dust and his new car without even trying. I smiled briefly at the thought. And then I had a sobering thought...what would happen to my home and land when I passed on? I suppose I shouldn't worry about such things. Such things I have little control over.

{Mr. Fennick pauses the telling of the story and when he resumes, the wedding is over and he is talking about the event.}

The wedding was a beautiful, if not a bit superficial, affair; a lot of money spent but not much feeling to the ceremony. I don't know that I really believed they would make it. Nevertheless, I loved my granddaughter and I knew she had her own path to follow, her own life to discover.

As I sat in the bright sunshine on the bench outside watching the people mill around eating cake and drinking champagne, I began to think about a past time...long ago when I was just a boy.

Gradually, I became that mischievous boy again. I could imagine hiding under the tables with their long tablecloths and listening in on conversations. I pinched the pretty girls and ran away laughing. This was a fun distraction to the noise of the wedding until I saw *her*.

At first I could not believe it...her back was turned to me, but I knew. She stood alone while the people around just walked by, her knee length peach dress swishing slightly as they passed. She turned, slowly, as if she could feel my gaze; her eyes downcast. I saw the silhouette of her face, long brown curls framing ever so sweetly. She lifted her eyes as if no one else existed and looked directly into me. There is something to be said for the strength that a look can hold.

I stood up and stared at her in disbelief and happiness. My wife, long lost love, had in a blink, moved across space and time and appeared immediately in front of me. She was smiling...not just with her mouth, but with her whole body. As I searched her face, I could see that her hazel eyes still held the love that I had always known. She had been my best friend and I had missed her so much. Nonetheless, it had been so long since I had seen her. What should I say to her? What was to be the right way to get reacquainted?

I brushed off my suit, secretly drying my wet palms, and offered my hand. I asked her if she'd care to dance; though I couldn't remember the last time I had danced. It didn't even cross my mind that I might not be able to.

She blushed, but placed her hand in mine and I had the most wonderful sensation run throughout my body. We stepped forward through a gathering crowd of people and out to where the band was playing. Elation, freedom and joy were the only feelings I experienced. After a moment, my young beautiful wife looked at me and said, "Mr. Fennick, dear heart, it is time go home."

{Mr. Fennick did not realize that he had just crossed over the threshold of death. For him it was a dream come true to meet his wife again after so many years. I feel certain that he will choose to be born again, and hopefully he will live a long life full of happiness.}

The paramedics spoke to my granddaughter as they put the body onto the stretcher. It had served me well and I was sad to say goodbye to it. However, being so old, it had become a kind of prison. Having a body for so long is like breaking in a pair of shoes and keeping them until seams come apart…it's going to be tough to do that all over again the next time around. I've found that sometimes the shoes break you!

{The final part of Mr. Fennick's story was given to me as a motion picture with some commentary as I watched.}

The guests told the paramedics that Mr. Fennick had been staring into space, looking into nowhere when he suddenly stood up and smiled a big ridiculous smile. They said that he mumbled a few words and reached out his hand. Shortly thereafter, he fell backwards heavily. The paramedics knew that there wasn't much hope for that body to survive as they tried to start IV fluids. Sunstroke and dehydration was the formal cause of death when they called time at the hospital.

I know better.

"Nanny" Leota
1910 in the Mid Atlantic Region of the United States

As she stood in the doorway of her home, she simply said that she was waiting for her husband to come home from work. Though I was with her in spirit form, she treated me like a neighbor who had come calling for tea. Be that as it may, when I looked around her house, it was as if I saw two different levels or times - one reflective of how she saw it and one reflective of reality. Her version was a neat and very well-kept house. On the other level I saw deterioration and emptiness; a shredded curtain blowing out of a broken window. It was an abandoned house.

There was a sense of confusion when I met Nanny in the morning hours of May 25, 2009. By this time, I had met enough visitors that I knew she was real; other dimensional. I was just unsure of why she had come.

I have, on occasion, met passers-by in my dreams– and by that I mean people who are not dead but traveling – like out of body experiences. Many times these people are physically not able to travel and are looking for any-one who will listen.

For example, a woman stopped by late one night to talk about food. She appeared to me as a beautiful young woman, yet, as our discussion advanced, her true form appeared. She was not a healthy person. She eventually told me that she was in the hospital for an eating disorder. She was so sad and discouraged; I listened and offered encouragement. When she left, it was in light.

For me there was no indication that Nanny had passed on. I can only assume that because she wasn't aware of her death I hadn't been aware of it right away either. It was the first time this had happened, and I was to learn that not all people who pass away realize it.

I was also surprised by her insistence on communicating with me. Never before had I experienced a visitor that stayed with me after I had started my day. She would follow me around and try to gain my attention by touching me or patting my shoulder as I went about my daily business. This was never anything that had happened before, and it is something to become accustomed to; to know and accept touch from someone who is not physically there.

Finally, as I was standing in the shower washing my hair, I closed my eyes and saw her standing in the shower with me. That was shocking. Then heard her clearly say, for the hundredth time that day it seemed, "let me tell you about my cats." It was enough for me and I spoke out loud to her, "I'm busy at the moment, but why don't you come back a little later tonight." To my surprise, she faded away and we continued her story later that evening when I was ready. I learned that I do have control over some aspects of the visitations.

The following is an account of my experience with Nanny that occurred over a matter of six weeks or so. I've written the story from her perspective.

Pay Attention

My husband is due home anytime. He is a trainman and is gone sometimes for a week at a time. I am so lonely when he goes away, but we have many homecomings to make up for it. I'm waiting for him now.

I sit here on our porch, which has exactly three big steps down to the sidewalk and five big steps to the gate, and I sip lemonade and watch for my darling to come home. The cold droplets of condensation run down the sides of my glass; I try to guess which one will run next as I patiently wait. My cats do like to lick the outside of the glass and would drink the lemonade for sure if I let them!

We have a small white-washed house that reminds me of a cracker box. I do get annoyed though, because as hard as I try not to, I occasionally brush up against the side of it and get white smudges all over myself. We put a new black roof on two years ago and painted our mailbox black to match. It is very convenient as we hung it right next to the front door. Our postman is ever so glad that we don't have a dog!

We also have a small garden in the backyard sectioned off with railroad ties; rather fitting don't you think? I am especially proud of the white picket fence that surrounds our house – even the front yard – that helps to keep out strangers and stray dogs.

The rail yards aren't so far away that I can't hear the comings and goings of the trains and their whistles and groans. It is a comforting sound to me; not at all bothersome because it signals the departure and arrival of my husband and the crew with whom he works. He is always so covered with coal and soot and dirt when he arrives, but I don't care; I always meet him at the gate with a kiss.

{Part of my work with Nanny was simply listening to her tell me about her memories. Some of them were general in nature while others were very specific. I was able to converse with her and ask her questions. I avoided anything negative, simply asking open-ended questions to stimulate more conversation.}

One sunny day when my husband was away working and I was pulling weeds in the garden, I heard the distinct soft crying of some poor animal coming from the alley. I took off my garden gloves and stood up, listening hard for the sound. I walked to the alley and heard mewing. The pitiful sound was coming from one of my neighbor's garbage cans. I looked around smartly before striding over and promptly digging in their trash. Oh, how my sweetie would have laughed at seeing that!

All of a sudden, my neighbor's black dog (who is always tied in the backyard) started barking. It scared me half to death! I could hear his owner yelling from the window for him to shut his trap. Along with the flies and rotting mess of peelings and the like, I found a potato sack of squirming little bodies. I grabbed it quick and got a wiggle on back to my yard. I could still hear that dog barking as I took my shears and cut the burlap open…there were six tiny kittens inside that still had their eyes closed. Someone had thrown them away. Well, tell it to Sweeney!

I took them straightaway inside and put them in a small basket with a warmed blanket. Of course they smelled so bad I had to give them each a bath. I just took a washcloth and wet it down a bit as I wiped their tiny little bodies like their mother might lick them. I think they really enjoyed it. It was so sweet the way they wriggled around complaining and looking for something to eat. They were so hungry! I fed them fresh cream with a medicine dropper every day, many times a day, until they were old enough to lap it from a dish. The first time they tried, they snorted it right up their little noses and sneezed it out all over the place! What a wonderful nuisance they were!

I watched them grow bigger every day. They knew me as their mama, for of course, I was. They followed me everywhere and listened to me talk as I went about my daily chores, hanging laundry and sweeping. Mostly they were little pests (and I say that affectionately) that pulled down my laundry so they could get to the clothes pins. And don't get me started on the sweeping…one or two or more of them would attack the broom and pull the straw right out – and then fight each other over it! Some days I couldn't sweep anything except little kittens!

Thank goodness they found distractions with grasshoppers and moths as I tended my vegetables in the garden and even managed to look concerned as I cursed the rabbits for eating my lettuce. My goodness, but I'm sure they could understand every word I said! More than once as they grew up did they bring me baby bunny tails and sparrows…little gifts left for me at the back door. I never once ate one, though on more than one occasion I pretended to, just to make sure they saw that I knew how delicious it tasted.

Of course they all needed names and we tried to match them with their personalities. Sissy was a brown-striped tabby with a shy disposition. She was also the smallest. Charlie looked a lot like Sissy but they couldn't have been more different in personality. He was quite independent and a very good mouser. While Sissy preferred to sit next to me on the couch as I knitted, Charlie would be on the floor taking swipes at the ball of yarn, rolling it all around and attacking it so that it was nice and wet as I knitted it into my blankets.

Taffy was a calico girl, mostly white with orange and black patches, who spent a lot of time in the kitchen. It is no surprise that she was also the fattest. Oh, how she would beg to get some bacon grease mixed in with her food!

Sugar was all white with one black paw; her front right paw. She was my husband's favorite. She would raise her paw when he came home or left for work...almost like waving hello or goodbye. She never missed a single day of seeing him off or home. He named her Sugar because she was very sweet. He could pick her up and lay her on her back to rub her tummy. Much as he liked her, he still said I was the Cat's Meow!

Dolly and Danger were both inky black and absolutely inseparable. Where one was, the other was sure to be near. They would curl up and sleep together at the end of my bed, and be so close to each other that it seemed they were one giant cat with two heads! They were pleasant enough during the day, but seemed to get into much mischief at night, long after I went to bed. More than once did I awake to a mess caused by nothing more than shadows.

{The more that Nanny and I spoke, especially about the memories she enjoyed, the easier it became for her to tell me about memories she had forgotten about...almost as if she didn't know they had existed. Sometimes she was surprised by what she said – and the pieces of her life began to come together.}

Eight years had passed since we had said our vows. We slipped easily into a comfortable life rhythm. We were very content, except that we still had no children. I began to lose faith that we would ever have any. My husband kept a light heart and believed that as soon as we gave up hope then I'd get pregnant. I was angry with him, that he did not seem as upset as I was... and as time marched on and I didn't get pregnant, my mood substantially worsened.

All of my kitties spent many days napping on the porch and laz-ing about the garden. They stayed close and did not wander as most cats do. I think they knew that I needed them just as much as they had needed me.

{Nanny's memories were somewhat incomplete – and she started to realize it. There was a lot of pain connected with the hope for a baby that never arrived. At times, I would pause our conversation and send her light and love. When her energy strengthened she would continue. At times we would go several days between meetings.}

Time passes so very quickly and my adorable kitties all grew up. My little Sissy came home today and brought me a big surprise, or rather eight little ones. They are precious. She carried them onto the back porch, one by one, and nestled them into a blanket next to the clothes basket. I know we can't keep them all; perhaps just one or two...

Oh, well, you know we kept them all.

{I hadn't spoken to Nanny for a whole week when she conveyed the following memory to me. This was very hard for her to do. It seemed that she knew by telling me this memory we would be unlocking the next part of her life...maybe she would finally understand why she was always waiting. It seemed that time in some sense had begun to pass for her and she was no longer satisfied with her circumstances.}

I fell asleep on the couch one evening. Something woke me up, but I'm not sure what it was. I looked at the clock, it was very late. I lay there for a moment and listened. The cats just watched me through half-closed eyes...except Sugar. Sugar was staring at the door like someone was there. She even raised her paw... it was so odd.

I called her over to me and spoke to her. I'm not sure what I said, I just know that I pet her until she fell asleep purring. This comforted me some-what, but I didn't really want to go to bed because it was such an empty place without my husband. I lay back down on the couch with a shiver, covered up with an afghan and fell into a fitful sleep.

{Another week had passed before she visited and again, it was very difficult for her to tell me what had happened. So much emotion made it hard for me to listen without feeling some of what she had been through. I cried, even though I don't believe I am meant to participate in others' memories. I think she felt comforted to share her grief.}

My husband didn't come home. Sugar watched the door every night. She would raise her paw after a time and then find a nice comfortable place to sleep. I think she was heartbroken...just like me. My husband never came home again. That was in 1936. Sugar died in the autumn of 1956. She was 23 years old. I hope she found my husband and all her brothers and sisters in heaven. I don't want to talk about this anymore. I am truly alone now.

{This was new territory for her; she hadn't remembered these memories at all until she had told me the previous stories. Her personality came to show through more and more – like she was finding her unique sense of self and letting go of the same old patterned history.}

I'm not really sure how many kitties I have now...at least seven and they do favor their mother. Sissy has been gone for a long time now, but I have seen her kittens have kittens and so on and so forth. Really it is quite comforting to me to see them running around, though it has not been good for my poor curtains.

Recently, there has been a new ragtag gang of neighborhood kids playing rather loudly in the streets. I've been watching them in the evenings from my porch playing "kick the can". There are two little girls who moved in next door that are a bit too young to play with them. They always seem to want to play but really are too shy. I'm glad that they aren't out playing with the boys; it wouldn't be proper.

{The healing process is in full swing from this point forward. Her attitude is turned toward the future and away from the past. Her inability to have children had such an impact on her life; she starts to make new realizations.}

This morning I saw the two little girls playing tag in the yard next door. I had dug a flower bed along our shared fence line late last year and had set about weeding it. I was expecting a proliferation of pink peonies to spring up this year. As I was pulling and digging out grass and dandelions, I noticed that the giggling and squealing had stopped.

I was on my hands and knees, and when I leaned up to stretch my back I noticed that the girls were standing right on the other side of the fence watching me very closely. Their cute little faces were framed in between the white slats of the fence, one above the top plank and one below, each holding on with the tiny child hands. I sighed.

What I would have given to have two sweet children such as these. Yet, I smiled, answered all of their many questions (and there were a lot), gave them some too-big gloves and promptly set them to work with me. You know my mother used to say, "If the devil catches a lazy girl, he'll set her to work at mischief." Around my house there is no time for mischief and always plenty of work to do.

Little Susie is ten years old and her sister is six. It makes me happy to have company, though in a way I am sad because I have no children. But there is something in a child's eyes, light and acceptance...because they don't know what you do about life...there is an unmistakable joy. Parents should never take that joy from their children; only too soon will they learn about life and its realities. Let them be children while they still can. I feel more comfortable around them than anyone else. I do so enjoy their visits and find myself looking forward to the next.

This past Mayday, little Susie picked violets and dandelions and put them in a jelly jar on my porch. I could hear her and her little sister giggling from the bushes next to the house. They had knocked and ran away. Good girls.

My peonies became "our" peonies and they did grow and sent up many big round buds. Of course there were a lot of big black ants crawling on the buds and this seemed to disturb the girls. I explained that there was a purpose for everything in the whole world; sometimes odd partnerships where each party benefits.

Though it seemed to the girls that the ants were selfish and only wanted the juice on the flower buds, in reality, the ants provided protection to the flower buds by biting and throwing off other insects that would hurt the plant. So, sometimes you might see something and think badly of it, but until you see the whole picture, it isn't what it seems...that you have to look at the situation in more than one way...and sometimes it takes someone else's view to help you understand.

And now I understand.

We were very pleased with the way our ants protected our flower buds, so much so that we would put sugar water in a jam jar lid and set it out under the flowers to say thank you.

{Breakthrough made. The lesson she needed to learn has been learned. The problem is that she still does not know she is dead – the thought has never occurred to her. I think she lives in her memories, though I know she cannot stay in that energy forever. I need to help her move forward, so I start to ask questions to trigger further memories.}

Time never stops. I have silver hair and wrinkled skin from too many sunny days in the garden. I thought today was Sunday, but when I looked at the calendar it was Thursday – and it was May, not March. I'm getting old – that must be it. Had to happen sooner or later. I fall asleep on the couch a lot these days. I just get so very tired. Sometimes I get terrible headaches. The doctor says I just need to slow down, but my kitties and my gardens do keep me busy.

My neighbor is very kind to me and takes me to the store and doctor when I need to go. I cut fresh flowers for his kitchen table and share tomatoes and peppers as they ripen. He is a gentle man and my closest friend. We sit on my front porch, sip sweet tea and talk about a great many things. His wife has long since passed on. She was a lovely woman, and also Susie's mother, who died in a terrible automobile crash in 1943.

{As she returns to these memories she goes through periods of confusion and thoughtfulness. She also realized that the man who was her neighbor truly did love

her...and she also appreciated his company more than she was able to admit. She was never able to accept his love in life because of her total reluctance to let go of her husband.}

We expanded our flower garden. It now runs down the entire length of our yards on both sides of the fence. Susie still comes to help me weed the flower bed. Her children call me Nanny. It sometimes makes me cry. I prefer this name because it has meaning...it gives me standing as someone important in their lives. I matter. Even though Susie and I lost those close to us, we helped one another. In many ways, I consider her the daughter that I never had; and I hope she considers me a semblance of the mother that she lost.

{After the final memory of her relationship with Susie unfolded, Nanny became more satisfied with her life, though she started asking the questions that eventually led to her departure from this Earth.

A few nights after writing the last entry in this story, the final chapter unfolded for me in a dream. Leota's husband had visited her every night after the rail accident which took his life in 1936. He tried to communicate with her through Sugar, but Leota never really understood that it was him that Sugar saw every night. It complicated matters when Leota died in her sleep from an aneurism, revealed to me through pressure in my head and the facts surrounding her loss of time and its passage; it explains some of her confusion.

When she did come out of the darkness, she did not realize she had passed on. She was very confused. Still, every night, Leota's husband would visit her. He would come through the front door and to us it would seem that he was an orb of light. Leota could not see him in this form, so even though it took considerably more energy, he started to take the form to look just as he used to when he was alive. For some reason, she was still not able to see him — they were simply on different planes of existence. It saddened him greatly to see her lost in this way...lost in the fog of memories and sadness and what once was. In her confusion she could not remember anything.

Last night, on June 23, 2009, I saw Leota's husband come through the door, as usual, as an orb of light. Leota was waiting for him this time and she saw this, too. He shifted into his human light form right before Leota's eyes. It was as if, for the first time, she was expecting him. I will not forget how her eyes shone with recognition and love as he embraced her for the first time in so many years of waiting. They had their final homecoming as he swept her in a brilliant light to the other side.}

Little Miss Mattie

1915 in the Southeast Region of the United States

Mattie came to me on June 24, 2008 during a visit to Siesta Key, Florida. In the early morning hours, just before dawn, she showed me a glimpse of her brief life. Furthermore, she revealed her death. Her message to me was not a clear verbal delivery, but rather a collection of images and feelings. Many times, it was as if I were her, going though her experiences, even as she died.

Unfortunately, her visit was difficult for me to experience. I woke up that night coughing and unable to breathe. The feelings we shared were frighteningly real for me. I wondered why this dream was so vivid? Then it occurred to me that I might ask what it is that she wanted. It became clear that she had wanted my full attention. As I lay back down to sleep, a story unfolded.

I awoke the next morning to stormy weather; a grey sky with fierce winds and lightning flashes out at sea. Mattie's overwhelming sadness at her life's unfair and sudden end pervaded my morning. My heart, now open to those voices willing to speak to me, ached with her grief. I thought of my own teen daughter.

Mattie's spirit lingered near mine for the entire day. The electricity in the air seemed to enhance our connection. She wanted to be certain that I would share her story, the essence being that we sometimes never know how much we are loved or by whom. I walked in the ocean surf the following day and as the sun sunk low on the horizon, I felt her spirit, accompanied by the loving energy of another, depart.

Embraced by the Sea

My father was a wealthy man, I now realize, though at that time I thought everyone lived as we did. I did not know him well. He was a handsome man with dark hair and a thick mustache. He occasionally wore a pair of round eyeglasses that improved his scholarly appearance. He was smart and polite. I often wanted him to spend time with me, but he was always away, always working.

My mother was a beautiful woman, though not in any traditional way. Her eyes were large; mouth small and heart shaped, like mine. When she smiled, everyone noticed and couldn't help but smiling, too. My friend

Jack, our gardener, said that she was like a canary in a gilded cage; she sang beautiful songs, but we would never hear just how beautiful because she was not free. Some spirits, he said, needed absolute freedom in order to live happily and that my mother was such a spirit.

Her brown eyes were always just a little sad. Her light brown hair was streaked with gold, a testament to many days spent in the sun. She hated the umbrellas that were meant to shade us from the dangerous rays of light. She adored sunshine and the heat that came with it...she said that it chased away the chill found in shadows. She said that upon seeing me, it was like a solar eclipse, that's how much I glowed in her eyes! And then she didn't seem sad at all.

I wished for more time with her, but she never even had enough time to finish her daily social callings and list of things to do. Most of the time that we were able to spend together was on the beach lazing the day away. We didn't have many of those days, but I remember them well.

Our family hosted lovely parties. They were usually held in our court-yard garden under the bright moon and stars. I was allowed to stay and visit with our guests until the sun disappeared below the waves of the horizon. It was then, as the sun set in yellow, orange and finally purple that I watched the dancing couples below from my bedroom window. I could smell the sweet jasmine wafting on the air and hear the musical laughter of the women below. Even as I lay tucked in my bed, music carried on the breeze through my open window, lulled me to sleep.

I was an only child. I tried very hard to please my parents. Of course I had to study classes like Etiquette and Elocution and Literature. I tried to be very grown up when they were near. Our guests always marveled at what a bright child I was and how well-mannered. I was very proud.

I lived in a beautiful white house. We had a cook and maids and I even had a governess instruct me at home. My favorite color is blue, though green is a close second. Alice's Adventures in Wonderland is my favorite book. It has a picture of a Cheshire Cat and a White Rabbit... it is so funny to see a rabbit wearing clothes! I have a small grey dog named Teddy, and I do secretly put dolls clothes on him. He is absolutely adorable!

I also keep a collection of tiny glass menagerie animals that I greatly prize. They are my afternoon daydream companions. Nevertheless, I am lonely. I often wish I had someone to play with other than Jack, though he is a very nice man. He just has so much to do.

I admit freely that I steal him away, even when he has things to do, in order to play with my collection of animals in the garden; we pretend that the world is magnificently large and that they have wonderful adventures in exploration! I also admit that I have caused him to get into trouble, though he refuses to allow me to say anything. I think of him as family, like the big brother I always wanted. He watches out for me.

{The energetic pace of Mattie's story slowed greatly at this point as she considered how to breach the subject of her death. She was in some distress because I don't think she had yet recovered from the flood of emotion she had experienced.}

I went to the beach alone that day. I had grown up with the ocean nearly at my doorstep, so I did not fear it. I know now that I did not hold a proper respect for it either. The waters were always blue and sparkling to me and very inviting. I even found it beautiful during a storm.

I was feeling sorry for myself, that I didn't have any friends and my parents were too busy for me. I sought comfort in the warm waves and soft white sand. And the Sea, she did embrace me as I glided into deeper waters than I ought to have swum in. I knew my parents would not approve, which is why I chose to swim so far out, past the sandbar at high tide.

It was a particularly beautiful day. The sun shone brightly overhead and the water was perfect. My swim was going well until something caught at my legs. I didn't know what it was and it surprised me greatly. I was suddenly being pulled in the water – not under, thank goodness, but my whole body was caught in a swift current going out to sea.

I was so relieved at first; that I knew it was not a shark. Though the more it pulled at me and the further it took me, the more worried I became. Soon, I could not easily see the shore and I began to fight it. It made no difference, it just made me tired. I now realize I made a terrible mistake... I should have swum sideways out of the current and then back toward the shore.

My legs were so tired. When the current let me free from its grasp I began the swim to the shore. I was afraid of sharks in this deep water. Fear compelled me to swim quickly. I remember feeling insignificant, a tiny speck in the big ocean. Time stopped for me. I could see fish in the water and seagulls flying in the sky – yet not one of them knew of my plight. My legs began to cramp. My breath came in ragged little gasps. Salt water burned my eyes mercilessly and I spat bitter saltwater back into the sea.

I had to calm down. I looked for the shore and still seemed far off. I had a long way to go. I tried to float for awhile so I could catch my breath, but I kept sinking. I was too afraid of drowning to relax enough to float. I looked at my house and could see small figures going about their daily business. They would wonder to where I had wandered.

A long time, it seemed, had passed. My parents would be angry with me. I started to swim again, the breast stroke, and I wondered if I would make it home in time for supper. I swam a little more before my head dipped below the waves a few times and saltwater burned my eyes and throat once again. I came up sputtering.

I kept going, just dog paddling, though I was very nearly out of breath. I paused and tried to touch bottom, to find the sand bar, but it was well under water now. My toe searched, pointed down like I was searching for sand dollars, when my head slipped beneath the waves once more – but this time, I held my breath, still going down searching for the bottom.

The waves pushed me around a bit. Then I looked up and it was beautiful to see the rays of the sun coming through the water…and then I felt shocked into reality. My lungs needed air. Badly. Fear crept in and panic seized me completely. I wasn't going to make it back…not unless I tried really hard.

I struggled to swim up when I saw the bubbles…coming from somewhere, traveling upwards. The water was warm, embracing and then finally smothering. I couldn't cough, couldn't breath. I was choking…all was just water – stinging my eyes and throat and lungs all at once until I pushed my way to the surface and broke through, gasping. I treaded water for awhile and then started kicking slowly toward the beach. This time, when I looked to the shore, I found that I had made it a little closer.

I don't know where my energy came from, but I began to swim with all my might. I even swam underwater. I began to think of myself as a mermaid with a bright green tail propelling me forward. It felt like I swam forever, but it seemed so much easier, like I was gaining strength instead of losing it. I finally made it to shore and collapsed in the warm sand. I was exhausted and fell asleep soundly.

I woke to the gentle sound of evening waves and my mother's sweet voice. She sat beside me, holding my head in her lap. The sadness in her eyes had gone. She wasn't angry with me. I could tell she had been worried. I told her I was sorry. She said that she loved me. I cried. She cried, too. I sat up and she hugged me close. Her eyes were wet with tears as she stood and pulled me up. She said she was sorry, too. I don't know why. We were happy, though, as we walked down the seashore in the moonlight. All was quiet and peaceful as the small waves washed gently onto shore.

{Mattie retreated softly away from me as I closed my eyes and allowed the pictures to unfold in my mind's eye.}

Jack, the family gardener, had become worried and gone looking for the girl and had arrived at the beach just in time to see her slip beneath the waves. He swam out far, risking his own life, but the girl had never resurfaced. He did find her and had brought her lifeless body back to shore. Local gossip in the area talked about the tragic loss of the girl's mother who, upon hearing the news of her daughter's drowning, immediately took her own life. She left no explanation behind.

Eli

1970 in the Southwest Region of the United States

As the dream thread begins, I find myself in a sickly pale green room with the paint peeling from the walls. I'm seated across from a young boy who is around eight years old. It's as if I am a social worker or interviewer and I have asked him to tell me about his home life, his mom, her boyfriend and his brother. He is sad because his younger brother, Samuel, is dead. He is having trouble understanding what is happening now and what has happened to Sam. Eli feels responsible for Sam's death even though it was an accident.

It is the morning of October 19, 2009 for me. I know that Samuel has already crossed over; it was immediate and he had guidance. Eli has grown up and seems to be in some kind of holding pattern. It feels like he is still alive though perhaps in a coma or deep sleep state. His physical body will not survive much longer and I think he will attempt to cross over soon, but is seeking some understanding and perhaps forgiveness.

The following story was given to me over two days and is told in Eli's own words. I have tried to make some clarifications throughout.

Responsibility

My mom works for a vitamin company. She really likes her company. She eats a lot of vitamins but won't give any to me or Sam...because she says we would be too much for her to handle. I don't know what that means. She and Doug, her boyfriend but not our dad, go to the gym and work out a lot. They are very healthy, I think.

Mom says they have a lot of customers at the gym so they make a lot of money there. She brings home big boxes of stuff and then she takes them to the gym and trades them for other little white super vitamins that she keeps in her purse. Mom says that they are way better than the others that her company makes. I think they make my mom feel really good.

My mom and Doug do eat a lot of super vitamins. It makes them kind of tired sometimes. Then Sam and I can do whatever we want. Sometimes we make sugar smacks, peanut butter and marshmallow sandwiches and chocolate milk for breakfast. That's when we have food, if Mom hasn't forgotten to go shopping.

We throw rocks at cans; and I'm really pretty good at hitting them. Sam likes, well, liked to play hide and seek. We always have the freedom, mom says, to make our own choices about what we want…so we should be happy. We don't really have rules except not to bother them when they're sleeping. So, I really have to look out for Sam…he's my little brother.

{Eli is looking down at the table, his shoulders are hunched, and I can tell that he's really sad about losing his brother. He does not understand that the little white pills were not vitamins but drugs…and seeing that I am speaking to the little boy right now, I know I will have to call in his grown up self. Before I could do that, he looked up and continued his story.}

You know, sometimes we would drive for the whole weekend. Other times, Mom and Doug would go away for the whole weekend and wouldn't even remember going on the trip! I remember getting smacked because they said I was making up lies. That wasn't fair, so I just learned to be quiet.

One time they decided that we should all go fishing. We drove out to the lake and started fishing from the dock. We didn't have any bait, but I had a shiny gum wrapper. Then mom and Doug drank some beer and took their super vitamins. Then they got really tired of fishing and Sam and I fished by ourselves.

We got really hungry and thirsty because it was sunny and hot. We caught some fish, but it was hard to take them off the hook. We knew that we accidentally killed one because we saw the blood coming out of its gills. It couldn't swim right and just floated on the water after awhile. That made us sad, but we didn't know how to help it. We got really tired and bored and wanted to go home. It was getting kind of dark before we saw mom again. They make me so mad sometimes!

Doug said he knew a shortcut to get home so I shouldn't be mad. He called me a few names and told me to shut up. He's so dumb. We were lost until midnight. It was so late that we fell asleep. It had only taken about a half an hour to get there. I got so mad at them. The radio was so loud and I remember that we hit something.

I think Doug is stupid. Sam and me don't like him very much. He never let my mom be by herself with us. Sometimes we just wanted to play with her. I wanted her to make my lunch for school sometimes because I hated mystery meat Mondays; but she never did.

{At this time, I interjected a question; what happened to Sam? I said, "I know you miss him, but I think you should tell me what happened that day." He just nodded.}

Sam got really sick before school that day. I couldn't wake mom up. I tried to wake Doug up, even though he might hit me for doing it. He just kept snoring. You see, I always get us up and ready for the bus; but Sam couldn't go to school that day. He felt sick to his stomach and was hot. I checked in the bathroom cabinet, but we didn't have any medicine.

Sometimes I have to take money from mom's purse so we can have lunch. That's when I thought that maybe mom's vitamins would help Sam to get some sleep and get better. I didn't know who else to ask, so I went to mom's purse and took out three pills because he was really sick. I stuffed them in a Twinkie and gave it to him. He wasn't really hungry but I told him if he ate it that he would feel better. So he ate it anyhow.

We watched cartoons for awhile, then, he just went to sleep. I stayed home from school and fell asleep on the couch with him. I was worried about him. I woke up in the afternoon. He just didn't wake up. He never woke up again...not even when mom tried to shake him. I don't understand why. I don't think I did anything wrong. I was just trying to be a good big brother. Now I don't have a brother at all. I'm so sorry!

{Eli was in such despair. I reached across the table and touched his hand. He looked up at me and I wiped away a big tear that was rolling down his face. He wanted so much to hear what I was about to say. So I looked him straight in the eyes and told him that it was not his fault. It was an accident. I also told him that Sam

was fine and that he would see him again soon. Eli's tears stopped and he heaved what seemed to be a big sigh of relief as he faded into nothingness right before my eyes.

When I looked beyond where the little boy had sat, I saw a grown man standing in the doorway of the room and understood this also to be Eli. He approached and sat just where the little boy had been sitting.

"My mom said it was my entire fault. She left me in the state's care; said she couldn't bear to look at me. People who looked at me did so with pity. I hated that look. As I grew up, I realized what drugs were…and I wondered why no one helped Sam and me. I'm sure someone knew what was happening. Thank you for writing this down. Thank you for listening. Maybe someone else will read this and take action to help someone they know. I'm relieved to tell someone, finally. I feel like I can go back now and talk about this with my group. You know we can do that, right? That we have a soul group we are a member of — and I have seven members in mine…I just didn't feel like they would understand. I think they are all so much more advanced than me now. I just can't wait to see Sam and tell him I'm sorry."

At this, a door, or rather a round glowing portal opened up in front of us. We could see what looked to be a great blue receiving room where people were having many happy reunions. There, waiting in the center of it all, was a little boy looking directly at us. It was Sam. He waved to us and smiled. I looked at Eli, who was utterly transformed into the young kid he used to be. He ran through the portal and picked his little brother up in a big bear hug.

Somewhere, in a hospital far away, monitors started making a lot of noise as Eli's heart stopped beating in this earthly plane. I'm not worried, though, because it seems he has just begun to heal. The portal sealed shut and the room went dark as the dream came to an end.}

Leslie

1995 in the Great Lakes Region of the United States

It's early in the morning around 3:00 AM on September 2, 2010, but I'm awake. I get up to check the house and as I leave my bedroom and enter the living room, I smell smoke. We have a fireplace, but it's the middle of the summer. I check the kitchen and the upstairs; no smoke.

I lay back down but it takes awhile to get back to sleep. This time, as I become self-aware in the dream, I see that I am staying in a lodge with a great room and huge fireplace. I'm standing on the stairs gripping the round wooden railing. I have no idea how I have arrived in this place at this time…I feel slightly confused.

I move past the staircase to check on the younger girls. They seem fine, except that one girl is missing. I go out of the room and down the stairs. When I reach the bottom, I smell smoke. The smoke is coming from the kitchen and it is starting to fill the room.

I yell at the girls to get up and get out. There's a fire in the lodge. I am a camp counselor at a lodge for girls; I'm fifteen but the campers are much younger. As the girls run out of the lodge, I turn to search the kitchen for the missing girl. She is there, hiding and afraid. As I walk by stainless steel appliances, I see a teenage girl with piercing green eyes and shockingly blonde hair that's bobbed short.

In this vision, I am Leslie, with her, and when I see this reflection, I realize it is her way of showing herself to me. I grasp at this moment that I am not her.

The dream continues as we move forward and fetch the girl who is too frightened to move on her own. The fire has spread quickly in the kitchen. There is no longer an exit from where we entered; however, there is a window. Leslie breaks the window and pushes the girl through. Then, with the fresh infusion of oxygen, the blaze in the kitchen, the heat and smoke, reach a new height and the dream abruptly ends.

{A day passes. I have thought about Leslie throughout. I'm unsure of what happened, however; I know it is not over. Leslie is such an incredibly sweet and giving soul that I find myself grieving for her…I feel I absolutely must see her again and try to help.}

The night comes and with sleep, the dream comes to me again.

A Repetitive Existence

I opened my eyes, already self-realized, in the dream state. I saw that I was again in the lodge standing on the stairs gripping the railing. I was swept with confusion at how I had arrived at this exact time and place once more.

Somewhat against my will, Leslie and I passed by the staircase to check on the younger girls. As we stood at the door, I wanted to root her to the spot so she couldn't move. However, as if on cue in a movie, we turned around walked away with the thought that the girls seemed fine, except that one girl was missing.

We walked down the stairs and on the last step, smelled the pungent smoke once more. Much as I tried to stop this seeming process, we made our way to the kitchen. Again, on cue, Leslie yelled at the girls upstairs to get up and get out. There was a fire in the lodge.

Leslie continued into the kitchen while I stayed put. Before long, I heard the window break and saw the flames engulf the room. I walked forward through the smoke and flames and saw Leslie's body lying on the kitchen floor. The dream abruptly ended.

The next evening I fell asleep quickly, only to be transported to the stairway once again. This time, I was accompanied not only by Leslie, but also by a grandmotherly figure with silver hair wearing a flowing black gossamer gown.

She regarded me quietly with her concerned green eyes. She said, "Leslie's been caught in this cycle for a while now. I've tried my best to get her attention, but nothing has worked so far. I've become somewhat resigned to the fact I cannot help her, yet I cannot leave her either. I've worn my best gown because this seems to me a darkly choreographed dance with steps and turns and an uninterrupted rhythm all of its own. That's why you're here; we both need your help."

With that, the scene began to unfold all over again. It was surreal as the silver-haired spirit took her place and began to dance to the ominous crackle of fire and hurried footsteps. Eerily, the timing of her dance coincided with the height and depth of her granddaughter's plight. The tragic dance ended in the kitchen amidst a crescendo of fire and smoke with her granddaughter's body lying motionless on the floor.

I willed the dream to stay in focus; I did not let it end. I reached down to Leslie's hand and pulled the spirit from her body. She stood before me, dazed as it were, and I asked her if she wanted to be free. She slowly nodded 'yes'. I told her, "You are choosing to be free, and so, you are free."

She stood before me for a few moments, just stood there…and I could not tell what, if anything, she was thinking. A slow smile of comprehension spread across her face. Grandma stood by me with clasped hands and a pensive smile. "It's time to go home, child," she said softly.

I felt deep satisfaction as the full realization swept over both of them. They dissolved into light, becoming small blue orbs and danced their way heavenward.

The dream ended and I awoke light and fulfilled in my spirit.

Sandy

2000 in the Midwest Region of the United States

Strangely enough, I had been experiencing some feelings before I actually went to bed on this particular night. I felt spacey and slow, habitually completing my nightly sleep routine without any thought at all. I became very tired; exhausted suddenly. As I closed my eyes, I felt some heaviness in my chest, some pain. I fell asleep and met my first dream ghost.

The woman clutched her arm and said she needed a doctor. She was standing in my bedroom in the dream. There was no animation in the woman's face or voice. She was empty, incomplete and somewhat transparent. She seemed a simple energy with only one thought looping through her mind; she needed a doctor.

The overwhelming impression that her guide imposed upon me was that the woman had thought very seriously about seeing a cardiac doctor recently, but she hadn't gone. I knew immediately that she had already died, yet she definitely did not know. Moreover, it seemed she was a shell of the person she used to be, a memory pattern with some thought capability.

She was still claiming to experience chest pain when she came to see me in the middle of the night on June 28th, 2009. Unfortunately, she had died quite suddenly at her home – so suddenly that she was still seeking medical help for her troubles.

Program Interruption

I asked her name, and to my surprise, she replied. She was interactive but running like a computer program. Most of her essence and energy had gone on and left a sort of ghostly memory of her human existence. I needed some way to interrupt the program, so I started to ask her questions. She was unresponsive and persisted with the statements of being in pain. I persevered and asked her to tell me the date, what she had eaten for breakfast, where she lived…but she couldn't answer any of those questions. She was unable to converse at that level.

Sandy's guide, however, was able to reveal through images that Sandy was a dedicated Christian with a solid belief in Jesus Christ. Indeed, she had believed in God and had prayed about her illness instead of seeking a doctor's assistance.

May I interject at this point and recommend that if you think you're sick or feel any pain, you should go to a doctor. If you believe in God, then you know that God works in mysterious ways and oftentimes his instruments are people and technology.

Sandy was a shell of a person existing in a shadow form. Her guide had been attempting to collect this energy and assist the process of crossing over, thereby completing Sandy's energy and essence to be whole. It had not been an easy task as Sandy was not in a state of understanding, yet she had enough will to stay on the earthly plane and seek out help.

I decided that a different approach would be necessary. I asked Sandy if she wanted to meet an angel. Her energy shifted very subtly, yet enough that it seemed to interrupt her pattern. I asked her guide for permission and then called an angel to us. It was not surprising to me when one descended into our presence. She was a beautiful creature with alabaster skin and rosy cheeks. She smiled and reached out her hand.

"Are you ready, Sandy, to go home now?" she said in a musical voice. The essence of Sandy reached out her hand and the angel drew her into a hug. Sandy's energy then dissipated from a form and became a tennis-ball sized swirling of grey and blue energy floating over the palm of the angel's hand. She used her other hand to cover the ball in a golden net of shiny energy before giving it over to Sandy's guide.

The angel smiled sweetly and flew away, I suspect to help another in need. Sandy's guide wasted no time, nodded his thanks to me and opened a wide portal that he stepped briskly through. The portal closed behind him. I have not encountered Sandy's energy again.

3

Hope From Ones Who Have Taken Their Own Lives

Hope and Renewal

Happiness is not something someone gives to you; it is something you have to find within yourself. It is a responsibility that we must accept in order to live fulfilling lives. Sometimes we have to work toward happiness as life does not always cooperate with our plans.

Unfortunately, people of all ages commit suicide; men, women and children and the rich as well as the poor. Why would anyone willingly cause his or her own death? It is because they are unable to find happiness, contentment or forgiveness within themselves.

Stories in this chapter help to show how suicidal people and those around them have felt from their different points of view. It is hard for us to understand a person's decision to end their life. We do, however, have to make peace with those decisions that were made out of our control. We can only control ourselves; this can be a very difficult lesson to learn. We cannot and should not want to control another person, yet, we should want to encourage good decisions and stop enabling the bad ones.

All of the people that made contact with me in this section have felt trapped by what they saw as hopeless situations. No matter the reality or emotional support that was provided by family, friends or even doctors, they still felt isolated and depressed. It did not seem that anyone was making a choice to die; rather it seemed that the choice became to end a painfully unbearable existence.

Suicide is such a lonely choice. Sometimes there are no apparent reasons. It could be a response to a physiological depression that goes undiagnosed. Many times it is associated with feelings of personal failure. We should always know that there are other options; suicide is never the only choice. It just happens to be the easiest choice; working through problems and issues is much more difficult, yet the challenge allows for personal growth and change. Once again, it always comes back to choice.

When someone takes their own life, family and friends often feel guilt and anger. These feelings are a natural consequence of the hurt and rejection we experience. We may feel that there was something we could have done. This is not usually the case, however; if you really think so, address it within yourself. Think about it and accept it but don't stay in that space; move forward. Your friend or loved one cannot be helped anymore, and you need to go on and live your life.

Should you feel that your friend or loved one still lingers with you, speak aloud and address them directly. Say what you need to say to make your peace and then tell them that they need to go to the light, to cross over, and get the help that they so desperately need. Ask them to go, for their health and yours, so that you can move forward in your life. You can learn from, and grow with, your experience.

When you care for yourself with respect and love, then not only do you attain happiness, you become a positive beacon of light for others. You are deserving of love and happiness. You matter. You will have an effect on the very energy that surrounds you... and that is attractive and will change your life.

Lieutenant Rico

1950 in the Southwest Region of the U.S. / Korean War

I was sleeping deeply, so deeply that when the dream transition into the story thread happened, I did not feel or note it. I started to become aware; like waking up after a heavy night of drinking – even still being slightly drunk. It was then that I tried to open my eyes and nothing would come into focus. It was too bright. There was a metallic taste in my cotton dry mouth. I tried to speak and it came out as a raspy whisper. No one was near. My whole body was in pain. There was a ringing in my ears, but no real sounds that I could discern.

At this point I floated up and out-of-body. I was surprised to see a man's body underneath me lying tucked under white sheets. He wretched and threw up. I became more aware. We were in an army hospital, make-shift at best. A nurse came by to help him and another checked the man's chart. It said the man's name was Lt. Rico.

I felt myself getting very heavy, slipping back down into his body. I spoke to him and told him it would be okay, that we were in a hospital and being looked after. I didn't feel him relax. Instead, I felt him tense as the memory exploded in his mind showing me the mine that had exploded under his feet.

As we shared this traumatic moment, I felt my right leg obliterate. I gasped and came out of the dream. I felt panicked and sat up in bed quickly so I could reach down and check for my own leg, which at that moment I could not feel. For a split second I even saw that it was gone, and then felt it return with a touch from my hand. It was there and I realized I was fine, though somewhat shaken. It was the morning of June 29, 2009 for me.

I felt that Lt. Rico was also going to be fine until I realized that he was devastated at surviving his catastrophe; indeed, he had stepped on a mine in enemy territory on purpose. The following story is told in his own words.

A Personal Hell

Some people do not believe an individual has a right to end their own life. Those people do not have to live an existence of constant and terrible pain. Our minds and bodies can be a prison from which we may never escape. The horrible pictures our memories record; the terrible sounds we can never forget. I will not say whether suicide is right or wrong; it is simply no one's choice but your own. You can accept it or you don't have to accept it; but you cannot change it. I speak to you on my own behalf and from my own experience.

I was eighteen years old, recently graduated from high school. Somehow, I ended up drafted to the front line fighting a battle against communists in North Korea. Who would have thought? It hadn't been in my plans. I had but stepped off the truck at the "end of the line" and was greeted by a sight I will never forget. There had just been a battle and they were carrying bodies away by the dozens. It wasn't clean or neat like in the movies; it was bloody. I didn't think we had so much blood in us. These were young kids like me; could've been my classmates. That was my first taste of war and I knew at that moment that I did not want to be there.

I was assigned to be a squad leader. It seemed they were a little short on leadership and I had been involved as a National Guard volunteer. There was no transition period for me; no time to get acclimated. From this point on, I couldn't remember any daylight at all. It was always dark. We were either standing guard or going out on patrols, but only at night. We slept fitfully during the day.

Not long after I arrived, my squad was sent out on patrol. Unfortunately, we were spotted by the enemy as we made our way to the top of a hill. All hell broke loose. I mean that literally. There were flares lighting up the night sky and explosions all around us.

Our squad became separated from each other as we tried to find any shelter we could. Shells flew everywhere. I dove to the ground and crawled into a rocky crevice to wait it out. Another soldier was already hiding there. When the dawn came, I looked at the man next to me. I had spoken what I thought would be my last words to him moments before and huddled close for protection. I thought he had been too scared to speak. I was wrong. It was a North Korean soldier who had been shot in the face. Death was up close and personal, like the stench that hung in the air, you could breathe it in.

It all becomes very personal when you see a soldier's eyes; sometimes you can see that they are just as scared as you and other times there is a shield guarding against looking at you as a human being. You don't know them...all you know is that you are supposed to kill them and they are supposed to kill you.

I didn't have it in me to stop seeing people as human. I felt sick to my stomach. I fell to my knees and got sick on the ground when I saw the dead laying all around me. There had been nine of us. I was the sole survivor. What a job it is to walk around collecting tags from guys you just had breakfast with an hour before. There is no dignity in this kind of death.

It was the beginning of my personal hell. I began to wish that I had been killed with them rather than trying to sleep. I kept seeing that enemy soldier shot in the face and the bodies of my squad lying in odd angles in the mud.

I kept going out on patrol night after night, never knowing what was going to happen. For awhile I wanted to go home and was really homesick. Then, it seemed, there was a turning point and I knew that I would never be the same again. That fact changed everything.

The fact was that I was "employed" by my government to shoot and kill communist soldiers…it didn't matter that some of them were just kids with guns. I knew they would kill me if they could, but how do you get okay with shooting kids that should be playing pick-up sticks or a game of basketball? They were that young. Nothing was right in this world I had come to live in. I just wanted everything to be over.

Was it wrong to begin to wish for the end? I didn't care what God thought…if he truly loved us then we wouldn't have been put in this situation. His divine will stopped meaning anything to me. His love was hypocrisy. Maybe God was just a lie and he didn't even exist. I really questioned it within myself. I just wanted no more killing. If I was going to die, I should be the one to decide when instead of just waiting to end up with a toe tag. After awhile, I stopped sleeping; I volunteered for duty. I lost my appetite and never felt hungry again.

The skirmishes continued. I would be on guard duty at night, hear the perimeter cans rattle and know they were out there plotting. It was torture because I didn't know what was going to happen. Sometimes nothing would happen, sometimes something would happen. I thought I would die of a heart attack long before a bullet hit me. I never ran away, though, I just planted my legs and stared out into the darkness taking one slow breath after another while my heart pounded so loud I thought the enemy could probably hear it.

I stopped wanting to go home. I would never be the same person that I used to be. My friends and family would not recognize me and I could not pretend to be okay when I was definitely not okay. It was all too much pressure to think about. I lost weight. I kept to myself. I didn't want to get to know anyone. I felt like a robot, but I did my job.

After a time, the guys in my squad started to touch me for luck. I had been out on over twenty patrols and come back without so much as a few scratches and a bullet hole in the stock of my rifle. I don't know how many men's lives were lost during those patrols; I didn't want to know… but I could never forget their faces. They could duck and cover and get themselves killed while I could stand up in the middle of a mortar attack and never be wounded. I began to tempt death and got a reputation for it.

My story became known to the company commander. He invited me to his tent one night for a cup of coffee. Instead of coffee, we drank whiskey. We spoke plainly; I told him I had no fear of death, indeed I desired it. He told me that because I did not fear it, death would not come. He predicted a long life for me and I cursed him for it. He did not care. He promoted me to second lieutenant and sent me to a place much worse than I had been stationed. Seems that crazy makes for a good leader.

My *new* commander ordered me to take my *new* squad and try to locate a sniper that had been picking off men at the fringe of the encampment. There were 17 of us. We struck out while it was still dark around five in the morning. I had ice water flowing through my veins that morning. I was numb. I knew something bad was going to happen. I looked around at all of the young faces, scared faces, barely out of high school faces…and I felt like an old man. I was the same age, but what I had seen had aged me beyond my years. I looked at those faces and saw death as a reaper stalking among them. How could I continue this life?

We followed the trails up and down in the pitch blackness, heading for the hill from which it was thought the sniper had been shooting. We reached the top of the hill just as dawn was breaking. We proceeded cautiously, not knowing we had stalked right up to a North Korean observation post.

We saw a low, concrete bunker that faced our encampment. The enemy were sleeping. There were slit-like horizontal openings that we could see within as we were only a few feet away. Our radio crackled. Heads popped up quickly in those windows. I don't know who shot first, but it was mayhem.

They threw grenades. They weren't smart. We picked up those grenades and threw them back inside their bunker. You see, they were throwing concussion grenades and the shock waves created by this grenade in an enclosed area do far greater damage than that produced by our frag grenades. We silenced them without much loss of life on our side.

My squad lost a few men in the fighting, but the bunker was ours. We stayed but for a moment so the medic that was with us could bandage up a wounded man. We weren't smart.

The North Koreans had been able to call in an artillery barrage on their own position. Mortar and artillery shells rained down on us. I stayed in my position. All of a sudden everybody was down. One mortar came in and hit the medic right next to me. He looked at me and said, 'Can you help me?' Then he died and I thought, why couldn't that have been me?

The attack stopped almost as quickly as it had started. Had it really happened, I wondered? Looking around I was the only man standing. There was only one other soldier still moving. I went to him. He was just a kid from Georgia. He asked me to put his helmet on his head. He was probably going to die. He had a big hole in his chest.

I don't know why I did it, but I grabbed him and threw him over my shoulder and headed down the hill. My balance was off and my ears were ringing. I fell down only to rise up again. I felt sorry for the guy I was trying to carry. I stopped for a moment and laid him down. He grunted with pain.

I had never felt so horrible in my whole life. I was in the middle of a god forsaken country, alone, in enemy territory. My squad were all dead; all but me. It was a blessing when I saw the partially covered mine on the path. It was my way out. No more nightmares, no more guilt or shame. Most importantly, there was to be no more killing or waiting to be killed. If death didn't want to take me, I would go to him on my own terms. I didn't think; I just stepped on the mine. Everything went black. Peace, I thought, had come at last.

They tell me that they found me close to that boy's body. He didn't make it, but they gave me a purple heart for trying to save him. That just adds to the guilt.

I woke up in a hospital. I know that I was not a very good patient. I was sent stateside to a hometown that didn't recognize me...and I didn't feel at home in any more. It's odd to see those familiar places and associate those memories to a person that you cannot even think was ever you. I was a stranger in a strange place. There was no place for me any more – nowhere to which I could escape. Memories haunted me every time I closed my eyes. I woke up at any little noise. More than once I grabbed my gun thinking I heard gunshots. It seemed impossible that I could be home when my dreams were so filled with darkness.

It seemed that people would shy away from me; it was as if they knew I wasn't quite right. Shopping, walking in the park; these normal activities caused me much distress. I didn't know how to interact with people any-more. Apparently, the things I said were not considered polite conversation and it really put people off.

My leg was gone. I was gaunt as I had no desire to eat. I felt like a freak. I didn't allow anyone to help me. I didn't want to be around anyone. No one could know what I had been through. I suffered in silence. No one could understand my personal hell. How do you explain it? Simple. You don't. I just chose to end it.

{We took a break at this point. He was very emotional. He had never spoken to anyone about his feelings and I could feel this release. Though he had chosen to free his soul from his physical body, his mind had kept him anchored here on this earthly plane. He had refused all help to cross over, though his guide never left him. He seemed stronger the next time we met. His guide was with him- and it seemed Lt. Rico had finally acknowledged him.}

I know you can see Atlas, my guide. I didn't want to talk to him for a long time, so I ignored him. He has been so patient with me. We spoke at length last evening. He said that there is no burden, ever, that we must bear alone.

If I had chosen to open my heart and look outside of myself, I may have been able to feel that peaceful presence that is always there for us. I was too angry to know that it was there, angry at God. I ended my life when I could have fought against the emotions I felt weighing me down. I could have tried harder to be with my family…even just to sit with them and watch them go about their daily normal lives. It just seemed like too much to share with someone else.

{There was another break at this point as he drew away from me. He was very sad and upset with himself. It was two days later when he drew near again.}

I came back this final time to say goodbye. I went to my parents and apologized to them. After all these years, I didn't think they would be able to feel me, but for them, I think, it is like I never fully left… there were so many unanswered questions. I asked Atlas to help soothe the energy associated with thoughts of me and my terrible exit from their lives. Though they are much older now, the pain is still fresh for them. I left a void in their lives.

I visited them in a dream, showed them a few happy memories of my childhood; a winning basketball game, a birthday party, my high school graduation…and I showed them me, waiting for them on the other side. I showed them me and I was happy, complete and fulfilled; there was no void.

They both have peace now…and they will speak with one another in the morning about their dreams. They will remember…and they will keep the peaceful feeling within themselves when they think of me. There is to be no more pain. They have suffered enough.

I go now, with Atlas, to my home where I can heal and understand more fully what happened to me in the last life. I still don't really understand; I maintain my hatred of war and that I ended up as collateral damage. I know that I need to work through some issues before I am born into my next life, and I will. Time does not pass for me. I know that I have all the time I need so I can recover.

{Rico, who had been wearing fatigues during all of our conversations, dropped the outfit altogether. His leg reappeared. He became light energy that carried a beautiful yellow hue. This was not an ending for him; it was a beginning. It was not a joyous crossing over, but a sober understanding that he had some serious work to do before he could return. Atlas, who was a huge presence, touched his shoulder lightly and they both faded away in light.}

Jonathan
1985 in the Northeast Region of the United States

Jonathan was a soft, frayed and hesitant energy when he came to me on the morning of June 21, 2009. He explained that he'd had second thoughts about talking to me…he didn't think that there was any hope that I could help him. I promised that I would listen carefully and write his story so that it could be shared with others. He came more into focus and he showed me a picture of his beautiful wife, Joan and nine-year-old daughter, Cathryn.

Initially he would not tell me his name. He was so ashamed that he had taken his own life. He was greatly saddened about leaving his family in such a sorry state of affairs. He sends his love and apologies. He doesn't believe that he should be forgiven at this point, but asks only for understanding.

He knows that he hurt his family beyond belief and he wants them to know that they did not drive him to commit suicide and likewise there was nothing they could have done to change the situation. Life for him had spun so out-of-control and he felt that he had screwed up so badly that he needed to end it, only it hasn't ended for him. He continues to relive his past and feel continuous guilt and regret.

Jonathan feels that he needs the approval from his family in order to start again. He needs to know that it is okay to move on. He knows that his wife has remarried and he is happy for her; yet he can still sense her sadness and confusion when she thinks of him – he needs resolution. He can see his daughter and the lovely young woman she has become; however, he knows that he will always remain a stranger to her...and it saddens him for it is not what he had planned. His story follows below in his own words.

Chasing the High

I had a cocaine problem. I snorted all of my issues away. I wouldn't admit that I was an addict in life, but the facts speak for themselves; I lied, cheated, stole and skipped work because of my habit. My addiction tore my family apart. My loved ones struggled with my problem not really knowing what was happening. They still bear the emotional scars of my addiction. I was never able to control myself, not after that first amazing high.

What had initially started as concern for me, sadly, over a rather short period of time, turned to anger and resentment. My wife didn't have to say anything. Her body language conveyed her an attitude of "Look what you've done to us". In life, I never saw how I had forced my family to travel down the addiction path with me; however each played their roles exquisitely. Even my best friend played a role; he was my betrayer.

When it comes to sharing the truth with someone who needs to hear it, no one likes to be the person to do it. Even when that person is just taking the most appropriate and necessary action, nobody really wants to take on the role – because it is not easy and not usually appreciated. Mostly, that person is met with anger and distrust. This was certainly what happened in my life. I know that now. I have known for awhile and have not been able to let go.

{With his initial statement finished, he took his energy to the background, like stepping out of the way, so I could watch firsthand as a story unfolded, as if it were a TV show. I will attempt to describe what I saw below.}

I was standing at the emergency door of a hospital. I saw a man, probably in his mid- to-late thirties, getting out of his car. He had the glow of health and an athletic physique. He jogged a few steps through the door and called out saying he needed some help for his friend.

The athletic man watched as the orderlies wheeled his friend into the hospital on a gurney. His friend was really sick. The stench of alcohol, vomit and urine emanated from him. It was obvious he had stopped taking care of himself.

As they began their initial examination the doctors noted his height at 6 feet and his weight at approximately 145 pounds. His skin stretched taught over his bones giving him the appearance of a skeleton mummy. I could see, though, that he had probably been handsome at one time. I was saddened at the sight. It was a terrible waste. It was then that I realized this was Jonathan and his best friend and betrayer, Brett.

As the ER team attended to Jonathan, Brett gave some details to a nurse. He said that Jonathan's wife, from whom he had recently separated, had been calling him for almost a week and had even stopped by his apartment. She had not heard from him. She had also received a several calls from his office, asking where he was and when he would be returning. His business partners had conveyed to his clients that he had merely taken a vacation – but they really were in a panic. It was then that she had asked Brett to go and check on him.

Moving backward through time, I watched Brett knock on Jonathan's door with no response. Wasting no time, Brett went around to the patio door and broke in. The apartment seemed in fair shape other than the reek of human misery. Empty vodka and whisky bottles lay all over the floor. The TV in the living room was broadcasting a cooking show. Jonathan was sitting on the couch, reclined; a skeleton reclining. Lines of coke were drawn out on the mirror that lay on the coffee table.

Upon seeing his former friend, Jonathan just looked at him and said in a raspy voice, "Funny, I don't have any taste for the stuff anymore," as he motioned to the TV. It was then that Brett made the executive decision to get his friend to the hospital. Of course, Jonathan didn't want to go, but what could he do? Nothing, because he was too weak…he was almost too weak to curse him out...almost. A lot of angry, hurtful things were said on the ride to the hospital; Brett still thinks about them and wonders if he made the right decision.

Things became clearer for me when I saw that Jonathan and Brett had been training partners. They had completed triathlons together; it hadn't really been that long ago. The demise seemed to have started after they had attended a charity event followed by an after-party. Both men tried cocaine for the first time. Brett walked away from it; Jonathan became lost in a jumped-up world continuously chasing the high.

Unfortunately, Jonathan could not see that he would probably never have as good a high as the first one and continued to do more cocaine more frequently just to feel all right. The friendship that had once been so easy became increasingly stressed, until one day it just ended. There was no more respect; not for himself and not from Brett.

Brett had watched Jonathan's life fall apart. He had tried to talk to him, as did so many others. The concern came across as intrusion and fell on deaf ears. Jonathan knew he had everything under control; or so he believed.

He didn't realize that he had effectively stopped participating in his family's life. He was too busy chasing other things that fit into a life of constant motion. With his marriage disintegrating, he had moved out of his suburbia home and into a cheap extended stay hotel. Prostitutes and drug dealers were regular visitors at any and all hours of the day and night. He spent every penny of savings he had worked so hard to acquire. He felt guilty about it when he wasn't high, so he tried to stay high. In the end, he was ashamed that he could not break the cycle.

Meanwhile, Brett had stepped forward and comforted Jonathan's young daughter when her dad didn't show up for her tennis match. Joan came to know him as someone she could count on. He listened and tried to comfort her. He came to care very deeply for this family in crisis.

As a single man, Brett had never found the love that he had once seen in Jonathan and Joan's relationship...he had never married. He saw very clearly that Jonathan was walking away from his family, his job, his friends...and there had been nothing anyone could have done to stop him. It hadn't been a logical choice for Jonathan; his brain screamed to stop, yet obedience to his bodily demands forced him to continue. It was a vicious cycle.

{The movie I had been watching pauses at this point. We come back to present time in the hospital. The movie begins again with Jonathan highly agitated.}

Jonathan refused admission to the hospital. His kidneys were failing and he had already experienced several mini-strokes that were impairing his ability to function. He didn't want treatment; he just wanted to escape to another high. He had stopped talking to Brett by this time. He was too angry at his old friend for bringing him to the hospital instead of just leaving him alone.

Brett called Joan and asked her to come to the hospital. She sat very uncomfortably in the waiting room. Brett stayed with her. The news delivered by the doctor was difficult to hear: Jonathan would need dialysis for the rest of his life unless he stopped drug use and was able to get a transplant. It was devastating. The drama was to continue with no end in sight. No one had known how dire the situation had become.

Jonathan would not give his consent for treatment. He was crashing from the binge and just wanted to go home. He was tired, depressed and angry. He really just wanted another hit to make the bad feelings go away. In reality, he had decided he wanted to die. He did not want to die at the hospital, he wanted to do it on his own terms feeling the rush of his last high. He told the nurse that he didn't want to talk to anyone and to please tell everyone to go home. As soon as the nurse left the room, Jonathan left the hospital and caught a taxi for his apartment.

{We pause here, for a moment and the movie stops. I can see that this movie plays for Jonathan constantly. He rewinds and fast forwards and watches it play out over and again. I tell him that this is the last time that he needs to watch it. I tell him that he needs to show me the ending that he has avoided watching. I offer him a few moments to compose himself and get ready for a change.

As he rests, I ask his angels and guides to come and surround him with love and support. I see him as a dull grey tattered spirit. As he rests in a soft vibration, I watch as he is surrounded by white light. One mighty angel with a great sword steps forward and begins to cut attachments and cords running from his spirit to the things of which he cannot seem to be free.

Another softer pink angel begins to gently scrub his energy with a wand of light. He is becoming lighter before my very eyes. The grey color is fading and I find that he is floating more freely. The feeling of the need to be punished is being alleviated. After a few moments, the angels stepped back and Jonathan continued his story}

I went home and snorted all of the coke in the house. I drank vodka; I don't know how much. I took pills; I don't know how many or what kind. The world sped up on a beautiful high just before turning really bad. Everything swirled together, mixed around me into a glob of colors and noise. I fell down and felt my chest explode.

The next thing I remember is that there was no feeling. I stood next to that broken body on the floor, not realizing for a long time that it was me. It was a wretched sight.

I went to my own funeral...sounds funny but it was very sobering. I stayed around because I still wanted to be a part of my family's life. I was angry that they were able to move on without me! In fact, their lives seemed better without me, except late at night when I would hear my wife crying. It was not me who would comfort her; Brett would pull her close and whisper words that I could never hear.

I made my choices, sorry as they were, and I have to deal with the consequences. I can't be angry with Brett or Joan any longer; hard as it is, I am glad that he is helping her. He truly loves her and I should be happy for them. It's still so fresh even though many years have passed. I guess it's time to move on. I don't need to say goodbye.

{The angels and guides who had been present had all left save for one small child; a little girl who looked to be four or five years old. She walked over to him and grasped his hand. She was an aspect of his daughter who was still living on earth. She said, "Don't worry daddy, we'll do better next time." Then she led him to a huge curved escalator that went up into the clouds. "It's a fun ride up," she said, "but the slide down is so much more exciting!"}

Haruko

2010 on the island of Honshu, Japan

It is night in my dream. I am flying low over the ocean, so close that I can feel the dark waves occasionally splash my face. I have been called to another place, so I travel quickly. I close my eyes momentarily and when I open them I am in a traditional Japanese home. Kneeling on the woven straw tatami floor opposite me is a young woman in her early twenties. She leans to one side with her head low and eyes closed. Dried tears stain her cheeks.

I ask her name. She replies softly, 'Haruko'. She knows she is dead for she has committed suicide. Her only concern is her son, whom she has left in an unsympathetic culture for children such as her son...he is not full Japanese. Her son's father is American and no longer in the country. It is the 19th of February, 2010 for me.

Hafu (Half)

I was wounded beyond what I thought possible as I watched my child growing up in my homeland. I did not, in spirit, leave him for a long time; though in the physical sense I left him to grow up without a mother or father who would love him.

Was he an American? Was he Japanese? Why did the children around my home throw rocks at him? Why were they so cruel and say that my son couldn't visit their homes because of the disapproval of parents or grandparents? He was but a child and could have no understanding of these things. Alas, I had committed an unspoken crime and loved a foreigner that I thought loved me. My child paid the price of my ignorance.

Our child was born out of love; however, I realize now that I was so blind. His father left as soon as our son was born. It became too much responsibility and all of a sudden I wasn't that fun or interesting anymore. My grandparents rejected their grandchild. My parents told me I was a huge disappointment and created nothing but a burden for them.

Where does one go with that knowledge? I knew what I had to do. It would be the only acceptable way to pay for my mistake. I had only one choice; how? Something that was easy and painless. Pills. Overdose. Just go to sleep and the nightmare would be over.

As I found out, the true nightmare began after I died...and I was not there to help. There was just so much sadness. But, through it all, I couldn't help but think that having my son was the right choice. I wrote him a letter to tell him so, though my parents never gave it to him.

I knew my parents would raise my son, but they would not love him; they came to despise him. As my son grew older, he asked my parents why he was different than the other kids, why his hair was lighter and why his eyes were blue. They did not lie to him. They told him he was hafu, that he was neither American nor Japanese and that he did not belong anywhere. It broke my heart to see him cry. I was not there to physically comfort him, yet I tried in spirit. He could not feel my touch through his pain.

He was adorable to me. I hated the culture that I had once loved. It prized honor above life. I had failed at life according to my family. I had failed at being responsible. My priorities had been wrong. I had believed in love. Love had failed me, I thought. Now I realize I had been a fool for a man that had failed me and true love was in the eyes of my child. I had been so naïve.

Though he sounded like all of the other children, he looked different, and he was different because he was treated differently. He was so desperate to fit in. He did have one teacher in grade school that pulled him aside and told him that he was teased because he had what the other kids wanted: large, wide blue eyes and sandy brown hair. She helped him realize that to be unique was acceptable…that you don't always have to be part of the group. I wish I had known her when I was alive.

On his high school graduation day, one of his mentor teachers approached him with a small gift and some words of advice. After all of these long years of watching him struggle, I saw him relax into himself after their conversation. As I listened, the teacher told him that he should not consider himself to be half of something, because that meant that he could never be whole of any one thing. Instead, he should consider that he was a whole of two cultures; that he could be a bridge between the two.

Then, that wonderful teacher said what I had so longed to say, that though life had been difficult, he could know that his mother loved him enough to give her life for his. She had lived and died by the old ways.

It was then that I realized all had not been in vain. My son was to help introduce a new way. It was a tearful yet happy conversation. The teacher had left him the gift, which was a small card to fit in a wallet or purse. It said, "Actions speak louder than words; be the change."

At that, I was able to start letting go. I look in on him from time to time, but increasingly find myself wanting to leave. I know he is fine now, and I wish to try again, to do better in my next life.

When my son started to travel and study history and different languages, he realized that his situation really wasn't that unique. There were many others like him. It had been very difficult growing up being different; however, as he grew older, it became more gratifying for him to be noticed as different. It was as if he realized that the world treasures that which brings us together as well as that which sets us apart.

My son is now married with a woman from India. They are very happy. When his little daughter looks at him after a difficult day at school and asks why her skin and eyes are different shades than those of the other children, he simply says to her, "You may wonder why you are different; one day, they may wonder why they are all the same."

4

Help For Those
Who Have Asked

Violent Acts

The stories in this chapter are disquieting and could cause you some distress. I know I struggled with the writing. I have nothing but respect for the courageous women who visited my dreams. They stepped forward with questions and difficulties as to why violence was committed against them. It seems that all of them were able to make some sort of peace before crossing over. The promise that I would give great effort to speaking their messages was requested by more than one; I agreed to do so.

Indeed it is hard to understand why we have such violence in the world – how can one person bring harm to another? Before we are born we may contract with others for a great many things, nevertheless, we do not contract with others for any kind of violent behavior. Violence is born from ignorance, laziness, and neglect; there is no pardon for this kind of behavior.

Elisabeth, my guide, tells me that when we are souls, we join with a human embryo some time after conception. We have several bodies on earth to choose from, in different countries and of different status. We work with our guides to try and choose the one that best fits our personality as well as facilitating our need to learn the lessons we have chosen. It is an agreement between soul and body; an acceptance to share life together. This is why, at times, we feel pulled to do things in body or in spirit. Each has its separate needs. This is why balance is necessary in body and spirit.

We can never fully know the ramifications of this human-spirit bonding. Physical bodies are bound by our physical world, meaning that they are prone to chemical imbalances, injuries, mental disabilities, diseases, genetics and other issues over which we have no control. A soul that may seem a good match for a body, in reality, may not be, especially given our soul's particular challenges. This is not to make excuses for violent behavior, for we all have choices to make and choosing light over darkness is one of them.

Stop and think for a moment. Your mind knows what killing means and can quite logically follow a line of reasoning to come to a desired conclusion. Your heart does not even understand the word "kill". Living and working from your heart is an expansive process that crowds out darkness and violence. Much more will be said on this matter later in this chapter.

Sarina

1965 in the Pacific Region of the United States

I fell asleep quickly on the night of May 18th, 2009 and traveled from the comfortable darkness of sleep immediately into a strange dimly lit stairwell. I was in spirit hovering over a young woman. I had but a split second before I saw the gleam of a gun in front of her and was pulled into the woman's body. A man pointed the gun and fired. I felt pressure in my neck and utter shock. Everything was confusing as we crumpled to the floor. Something on my hand felt warm and wet; then I saw the dark stain of blood spreading in a pool around me. There was a feeling of complete surprise. Then, the woman's voice, Sarina's voice, thought, "Oh my God, so this is how it feels to die."

She was horrified. I whispered to her, "You are not alone, I am with you."

There are No Coincidences

We watched the man put away the gun, take out a small camera and take her picture as she bled to death. It began to feel cold and dark. Sarina had difficulty breathing; it became very shallow as we struggled for more air. Subsequently, everything stopped and there was no more feeling or breathing.

I woke up at 5:00 AM unable to breathe. My heart was beating fast and I was afraid. I could feel my guide's soothing presence and I was comforted in the knowing that I was safe. I was able to take in some air and gradually catch my breath. I think I took quite a few deep breaths before feeling comfortable enough to try to sleep again.

Sarina was waiting for me to close my eyes even though I wasn't quite sure I wanted to know the rest of the story. Her tense energy was tangible in the room. She held herself in a small tight vibration; she was anxious. She had needed to get my attention, and she had; I was paying close attention. I asked my guide to watch over me and then gave myself over to sleep once again. It was a conscious decision to allow her story to continue.

For the first few moments of the dream, I floated above the scenes unfolding below. I saw a well-dressed professional young woman in the marble lobby of a nice office building. The woman had dark brown hair and smoky eyes. She was petite and lovely. Unfortunately it was Saturday and she was working.

A handsome middle-aged man walked up to the elevators, seemingly by happenstance. There was some small talk, scoffing about it being Saturday and the elevators out-of-order. Sarina walked over to the stairwell door. The man followed her. The door slammed shut with an echo.

The two of them were still making casual conversation when they reached the landing between the first and second floors. He was very charming and flirting with her in some manner. She was a few steps ahead, but turned to him as she was interested in this playful conversation. They did not know one another. He was commenting on the weather complying with dinner plans as he pulled out the gun. She did not see it. It had been fitted with a silencer.

The man was a professional and had been hired to kill her. He had been given specific instruction not to damage her face. She turned again to flash a brilliant smile at something he had said. He was not smiling as he shot her in the neck. He placed the gun into his jacket pocket and watched her shocked expression as her body slowly crumpled to the floor.

She grasped at her neck as blood spilled all over the stairs. She couldn't speak, but there was such disbelief and shock registering on her face. "Why?" she seemed to ask. The man took a small camera from his shirt pocket and snapped a picture. He shook his head slightly.

I could almost read his thoughts...a job is a job, but it's such a waste. If he'd had his way, he would have planned it differently. He would have seduced her and enjoy his victim for a change. It was a sexually gratuitous thought, even if she would not cooperate. The outcome for her would still have been death. He turned and left the way he'd come. The scene faded from my view.

This dream had frightened me. I decided it might be a good idea to call my friend Jacki, who is very experienced in spiritual matters, to get her point of view on what was happening and how to get control. As usual, she asked me a few pointed questions that brought me quick answers.

I had set no rules – and for every situation in life and apparently after death, there are Rules of Engagement. This was the lesson I needed to learn: that I always have control. After meeting Sarina, I put my guide in complete control over who was allowed to visit my dreams and how they were able to get my attention. From this point on, Elisabeth (my guide) was my Gatekeeper. This helped me to be able to go to sleep and not worry about what would happen. That didn't mean that I would never be uncomfortable again, or even that I wouldn't wake up with start, but I was able to start getting sleep again and recover from the late nights and early mornings.

Sarina has made peace with what happened to her and has crossed over, though she wants the person responsible for her murder to be brought to justice. She does not know who killed her or why. If you think you know something about this case, please write to the email address at the end of this book with your information and I will reply or forward if I feel so compelled.

Aubrey

1970 in the Rocky Mountain Region of the United States

I woke up angry on this morning. This never happens; sometimes I am contemplative or maybe even a bit sad, but never angry. It was November 11, 2009. I ran a shower, hoping the hot water would help me feel better as it usually does. It didn't. I continued with my morning routine and was about to comb the tangles from my wet hair. I stood in front of the bathroom mirror and the fact that it was steamed-over irritated me. I took a furious swipe across it. What I saw in the mirror startled and frightened me.

A man stood behind me with a fireplace poker raised; the blow fell heavy on the back of my head. My breath caught in my throat and my knees went weak as the memory of a visit that I had dream-experienced and forgotten that morning came flooding back. I leaned forward and rested on the sink as the pressure in my head receded. I closed my eyes and the scene came more fully into view.

The dream visit had been somewhat disjointed. I was with a young woman in the dream. She is leaning on me heavily, unable to support her own weight. Blood flows from her head down her naked shoulders; her hair still wet from the shower. I am concerned about getting her away from her boyfriend. I am walking with her, and she is so heavy...her feet are just about dragging.

I get glimpses of her boyfriend, angry flashes, and I try to move faster in order to get away. I'm certain that the girl is dead and doesn't know it yet. She had come to me to help her escape from an angry energy that still pursues her even after death. The following story was relayed to me during subsequent dreams. It is told from her point of view.

Knock-Out Blow

My name is Aubrey. I am 23 years old. I'm sort of shy, so I never really go out. I used to work at a convenience store so I could talk to people and actually make a few friends. There was a man who used to come in and chat with me. He said I was pretty. He said that I would make a good wife and mother.

One day not long after we met he asked me out on a date. I was really excited about it! I don't normally drink, but I drank at his insistence and was really feeling it. We were walking to the car after dinner at the restaurant. I remember that he asked my opinion about a pro-football team. I mumbled that football was a dumb, boring sport. I found out that he didn't agree with my opinion.

I don't remember the rest. I just woke up lying on the sidewalk outside the restaurant. A group of people walked by and I heard him say that I was drunk but fine. I realized slowly what had happened as I came around and felt my throbbing temple. I got up, bruised and bleeding from where I had fallen and stumbled away from him. I should have kept walking and never looked back. Instead, I ignored that little voice in my head.

He followed me, apologizing, saying he didn't mean to hit me. It was my fault, though, that he was angry with what I had said. I was really confused. I made a big mistake by allowing him to take me home. That was the first time, and it was a knock-out blow.

What was really weird is that the next few days were incredible. He acted like he couldn't get enough of me, so I gave him another chance. A lot of people get violent when they get drunk; we just wouldn't drink. We talked about what happened. He knew he had done something wrong.

He told me about watching his father beat his mother. Through streaming tears he declared that he wasn't going to let it happen to us. With such a new whirlwind relationship, I should have known better than to trust him. Tears do not mean anything; it was just a way to control how I felt. He was manipulative and I was very naïve.

He treated me like a princess. I moved into his house two months after we met. I left my mom's house against her wishes. Somehow she knew he was bad for me. She said I could always come back. I never did.

I know when the abuse began; only, I don't know why I stayed. I can still see his face; see the anger and hatred stamped on it. I always thought if anyone ever hit me, I would leave him immediately, but I didn't. It seemed a lot more complicated than that. I'm not sure why. As I look back now, I see that it's really quite simple. If someone hits you, leave. Immediately. And don't go back.

As time went on, the incidents became worse. He would say the nicest things to me until I disagreed with him or told him something he didn't want to hear. The change was quick and completely unpredictable. He would turn on me. It felt like he had two personalities, a real live Dr. Jekyll and Mr. Hyde.

He said I was stupid but I knew just how to bring out the worst in him. I learned a lot in those first few months; how to do as I was told, how to walk softly, how to hold my tongue. Only I could never quite get it right because I always ended up hurt.

Every few weeks I could feel tension slowly rising between us. Something simple would begin it; like me wanting to visit with my mom. He didn't like me to go anywhere or see anyone, so I accommodated his wishes and I didn't see anyone. I stayed in the house so he knew where I was all the time. If he called, I ran to catch the phone.

Of course, I had to quit my job. I hadn't seen my mom in over a month. It didn't matter. He still accused me of cheating, even though he knew I wasn't; it was just an excuse to get things started. He would shout in my face showering me with spit and I just took it. He would raise his hand and watch me flinch and then laugh at me.

One particular day I forgot to feed the fish, so he put his fist through the fish tank. He was screaming about responsibility as the water rushed out everywhere and the fish flipped around on the floor. Blood gushed from a cut on his hand; of course, it was my fault. I had to clean up the mess and tend to his wound. I wasn't allowed to save the fish. I had to sit and watch them die; that was my punishment for not feeding them at the proper time. His eyes just looked at me saying 'why did you make me do that'? Everything was my fault.

I was always nervous when he came home from work. Did he have a good day? I certainly knew when he did not. He would start drinking and with every beer he drank, he became louder and louder. When he couldn't get the response he wanted from me, he'd jump up and grab me. It was volatile and brutal. Once the initial blow was struck he liked to draw the beating out, taking pleasure in it. He would smack me around the head, screaming at me the whole time; although he would never hit me in my face. He punched my arms and thighs hard. If I ran from him, he would chase me through the house and corner me. I can still smell his reeking alcoholic breath as he breathed over me, twisting my arm behind my back, hurting me. He would leave me crumpled and broken on the floor like a piece of wadded up wastebasket paper.

That wasn't the end though, because every session was followed by sex. I would be suffering and swelling after a beating, forced to lie under him, bruised and utterly desperate. He talked to me, as I lay there, telling me that I knew I deserved what I had gotten. He said that he truly loved me and was doing everything for my own good. I had to say 'yes' and 'that's right'. If I didn't say it or act like I enjoyed what he was doing, things would get rough. Then I was truly sorry. I never wanted sex like this. I had wanted to be loved. After a time, we never had any kind of sex except this kind. I began to hate him, yet I still thought I loved him; I always feared him. What I did not understand is that if there is fear, there can be no love. If there is no respect, there can be no love.

My weight dropped dramatically. It had only been six months, yet I was black, blue, green and yellow all over. I searched for any kind of remedy that would fade the bruising faster. He didn't like to be reminded of what he had done. I went through cover-up at a frightening pace.

I had not spoken with anyone about what was happening. I had not spoken to any friends or family in two months. I felt so stupid. Although I knew this was wrong, I made many excuses. I was ashamed. I hated myself for being so dumb. I believed that I deserved what was happening to me because I was too weak to leave. I didn't have any money and I didn't want to go home to my mother and prove that she was right. Besides, how would I get my things?

Every time the abuse happened, he said it would never happen again. Every time I accepted his apology. Every time I felt stupider than before. I vainly clung to the hope that I could change him because I thought he loved me. I didn't know what love was. I thought I could fix him.

I tried so hard to be what he wanted me to be; but this didn't make him happy. I surely wasn't happy. I had forgotten what 'happy' meant...I had forgotten the person I used to be. I stopped having likes or dislikes; I just measured everything by how he thought and reacted. I survived by clinging to those precious few good times in between the bad ones. They were my glimpses into happiness.

Then something happened that changed my life. I accidentally broke the faucet in the kitchen. I had to be punished. I was banished from using running water in the house for a week. I'm glad it was springtime because I had to take my showers with the hose in the backyard.

It was early morning, and I thought no one would be about, however, I caught my neighbor's eyes watching me over our fence from her deck. She had seen my bruised and broken body as she sipped her morning coffee. I was greatly ashamed and rushed inside. I wondered if she would call the police, but no one came. Later in the day, when I was sure my boyfriend wouldn't be home, I went over to talk to her. She didn't say anything about the incident. She acted like I was just a neighbor coming over for a visit.

Somehow we became friends. Just chatting with her over tea and cookies made me feel better. She didn't want anything from me. She didn't tell me how to live my life or tell me what I was doing wrong; she just asked me some questions that I didn't know how to answer. It took some time, but I came up with the answers.

It felt good to have a direction. I think she was the reason I realized that life could be better and that I didn't have to live like I was living. My happiness mattered. I had options and choices. I called my mom and talked to her. It was the last time we spoke. She was happy I had decided to come home.

Things, for me, changed inside. I became brave with my sweet retired neighbor's support and told him it was over. It felt great but it was dumb. It was maybe the stupidest thing I've ever done. Nevertheless, I had decided to leave and had made plans with my neighbor's help and I had called my mom, so I was blissfully happy. He went to work. I laughed, sang, and danced while I cleaned the house for the final time.

He was so sweet when he came home that evening. He'd brought flowers and my favorite Chinese take-out for dinner. He asked me if I was sure I wanted to leave. I said I was sure that I needed some time away to think things through. He had nodded in understanding. He wanted to be together one last time before I left. I said okay even though I was repulsed at the thought. This was another mistake.

We stayed up late. I lay in bed afterwards, listening to the ceiling fan make that humming noise in steady rhythm. The curtain moved gently with the breeze of the fan. Soon enough I heard him snoring next to me, so I decided to get up. I wanted to take a shower so I could wash him off of me...for the final time. I took a really hot shower. My skin turned pink with heat, and gleefully, I thought, pink with happiness. I was so cheerful that I would be leaving in a few hours. I had already started packing. It was good that he had taken the news so well.

I stepped out of the shower and dried off. I wiped off the clouded mirror and my smile faded. There was my boyfriend with a fireplace poker raised over his head. I can't forget the look on his face. I didn't have time to say anything as the blow caught and I felt the pain in the back of my head.

I opened my eyes to find myself being wrapped up in the shower curtain. My God, this can't be happening. Things were fading in and out. I was being pulled somewhere. I watched the baseboards go by one step at a time.

When I opened my eyes again, I was in the garage on the floor; the car trunk was open. I tried to get up but was only able to turn my head. I saw his feet, and I looked up just as he swung again, catching me in the side of the head. He was quiet, determined, nothing but cold anger burning in those eyes. He swung again, and again, and again. It didn't hurt anymore. Is it over? Is this all that you have for me?

{Aubrey leaves for the night. Sometimes I can feel the energy of those who I am working with linger; her energy left completely. She returned fully the next evening. She seemed better, like talking about her situation had helped.}

I went to my mom's house last night. She was just sitting at the kitchen table, reading a book. I sat down in the chair next to her. She didn't even look up. I reached over and touched her hand. She's older than I remember, lots of worry lines on her face. I asked her not to worry anymore. I've been visiting her for awhile now...it only makes sense that I'm dead, right? I guess I've never really thought about it...it's too hard to think about. I've been running away from him for so long that I just didn't know how to stop. I think I can do that now.

I like the way that my mom is always so quietly absorbed in a crossword puzzle or Sudoku problem. We never talk. It's comfortable. I've just been hanging around, now that I think of it, to be with her and feel safe. I really hadn't thought I needed to go anywhere else. I didn't really think about how I got there.

I guess it's time to go and let my mom be in peace. As difficult as it has been for me, it's been a nightmare for her. She already knows what happened; that I'm gone...she has faced it better than I have. I haven't made it easy on her because I'm still here and I know she can feel my presence. She knew so much more than I gave her credit for...I only wish I would have listened to her.

There are people in this world who are ignorant and selfish. They don't know what they're doing or why. Don't be naïve. Protect yourself and trust that little voice in your head because you are worthy. If you are in a situation like mine, leave! Never tell them you're leaving. Just go. Don't worry about the money or the things you're leaving behind. That's all they are... material things. You can get more, you can make more, you can replace them; you can't replace your life. You are here for a reason; figure it out and don't give up. You are in charge of yourself.

{A bright white light shone down on Aubrey, making her look like an angel without her wings. She looked up into it and then back at me. She sighed, "You will tell them about me, right? I didn't die for no reason, right? Tell my mom, if

you happen to meet her, that I love her. I just didn't know what love was until now."
I just nodded 'yes' as she crossed over unaided into the light.}

Aubrey has never been seen again. Her boyfriend has moved to a different state and has left this past behind. He remains a murderer and is currently in an abusive relationship with another woman. He still has his freedom. You would never know that he is an evil man; he looks and acts the part of a normal good-natured person. Be aware that some people are not what they seem.

Lauren

1990 in the Mid-Atlantic Region of the United States

I am sad. I am floating above a spot of ground in a thickly wooded area. No one knows I am here. It is so very quiet; not even a bird makes a sound. As I look in the black soil and see the breeze bend the dark green ferns, there is a glimmer of white in my mind's eye. A portrait of a blond woman appears in my mind, though it is fleeting.

I hear a haunting moan caught in the wind. It quiets gradually, much like the breeze as it settles. There is a memory that lives here, a true phantom. I heave a sigh and feel the heaviness descend. It's crushing. All is still as she finds her voice. The energy emanating from her wavers from sad oscillating to angry and back again. As I awake, it is September 11, 2009.

Seeds of White

Can you see them there? Lying in the dirt like seeds that haven't sprouted? They belong to me. The only thing left to prove that I ever existed are my teeth. I think they look like white seeds lying in the black dirt, scattered with the leaves. I've been here a long time, though I can't remember how long.

I know an evil man killed me. I followed him after I died. I watched him pull out my white, polished teeth and throw them here. He hid them, hid me. I couldn't stop looking at them. It was a hideous process. I am still repulsed and terribly angry.

I stayed here. I'm not sure what happened to the rest of me, though if my teeth are any indication, I'm sure it was horrible. I'm so frustrated now, though, because I know I belonged somewhere. I just can't remember where. Someone surely remembers me. Someone surely wonders where I am…wonders what happened to me.

I need someone to find me. I want a proper resting place so that I can go to heaven…away from the wild things that roam here, away from the wind and rain and darkness. I am so alone.

{Lauren is in a great deal of distress at this point in our meeting. I did not want her to withdraw, so I asked her to stay with me in the dream state for awhile. She seemed locked in a cycle of frustration and despair. At this point, I'm not sure she really understood what had happened; it was hazy.}

Lauren's guide stepped forward, as I felt the energy shift, and was able to convey the most simplistic explanation; she had been taken against her will, assaulted, murdered and her broken body left in a great wooded forest in a shallow grave. The man who murdered her did not want her identified if her body should be found. I came to understand that Lauren knew what happened but was unable to truly face it. She was reluctant to leave her remains. She persisted in taking the form of who she was in life; though it was vaporous and wispy. Lauren looked every part the ghost. At times, I am sure the living has seen her as a ghost lady wandering through this wood.

We resumed our conversation and I assured her that she was greatly missed and that there are those who still look for her. I promised that I would help as much as I could. I asked her why she hadn't gone to the light. Her explanation was that she hadn't seen any light. She said she had nowhere to go and was satisfied to wait. It was a strange thing to say. Delving deeper, she said she waited for someone to come and rescue her – as she waited for someone to save her in physical life from the death she experienced.

I explained to her that she could save herself from this forever sadness of waiting; that she possessed the power to make the choice to leave if she wanted to go. She was very thoughtful. I don't think she knew where to go and was still disinclined to leave. I continued and conveyed that the forest was a natural cathedral; it was a most proper resting place. I told her that we could ask the wild animals, which she seemed to both fear and detest, to watch over this ground instead of being an antagonizing force. We could declare her resting place as sacred and untouchable; protected. At this, her energy shifted into a different vibration.

At this time, her guide was able to come fully into view. I've never seen a guide such as hers before; she seemed to be of the forest, leafy and glowing bright green. The glow completely engulfed Lauren. The ground began to glow beneath them. Several large white light wolves jumped from this portal; they patrol and protect this ground, even now, until Lauren's remains are found. Lauren's guide raised the energetic essence of Lauren from the ground, so that truly, the only thing left in that ground was her teeth. The lady in white no longer haunts those woods, though to anyone who passes, the ground seems hallowed. She looked like an angel as she ascended through the canopy of trees, following the light to the Other Side.

5

Incomplete Stories

Evil Does Exist

I want to address the concept of evil. While these stories may not be easy to read, they do contain some final messages and requests that will help ease the souls of those who have spoken and may give some peace to familial survivors.

Make no mistake, there is evil in this world. As with everything, there must be balance. There is good, so there is evil. It is a fact. We cannot control it, nor should we try. We can only take precautions and watch for warning signs. Listen to your inner voice and pay attention to how you feel. Your senses will help you to understand what is happening even if your logical brain does not understand.

If you feel afraid or repulsed by some person or place, do not ignore that feeling, pay attention and leave that situation. People who are confused, undecided or lacking in direction are easily led and influenced. There are low energies, negative and persuasive that will encourage a supposed "easy" way of living. It may start with stealing or lying, but with each acceptance and action, theses negative energies are encouraged and will become more influential.

Anger, mistrust and hate play their parts well and encourage violence. The possibility of the attainment of power in a world where people feel powerless can be alluring and motivating. At times, the soul housed within the body shuts down under the pressure and allows physical emotion and outside influences to dominate. Nothing can be learned in this state of being.

There are truly malevolent spirits in the earthly plane. Whether you call them demons or evil spirits or low vibration energy, their existence is not to be considered lightly. Take, for example, the Ouiji Board; it is probably not a good "game" for you or your family as it is an easy way to open the door to lower energies. Higher guides and energies will speak to you in your heart, mind and dreams – and will not inspire fear.

For many years I was plagued by a terrible nightmare. It was always the same concept, even the same people in the dream, and I would be terribly afraid in the dream and even after I would wake from it. Some days I would carry the memory of that dream with me as I completed my daily tasks.

I eventually realized that the dream was more than that; it was a staged condition for an entity that fed and was strengthened on the energies of fear and terror. It had discovered my greatest fear and was creating the perfect dimensional situation from which to take what it needed. It is a terrible feeling to know that someone or something can actually take pleasure and feed on another's terror.

Being aware is the first step; just recognizing what is happening and accepting that action must be taken in order to free yourself from the situation. No longer do I accept or suffer from such attacks.

Listen to your inner voice. Take precautions but do not fear. Fear attracts entities that feed upon fear. Be strong and ask for assistance if you feel fear. There is no reason for you to live with fear. The angels, guides and protectors that watch over you, whether you ask them to or not, are always present to act on your behalf. Say a prayer of protection over yourself and your loved ones each night; it will make a difference.

Furthermore, understand that every action we undertake has a consequence with far reaching ramifications. Our negative or evil actions follow us until they are made right. This continues through death, the afterlife and following lives yet to be lived. We do not control how fate decides to make a soul's actions right; fate will merely intervene at the appropriate time and make corrections unless the initiative to make amends is undertaken.

This does NOT mean that someone who is murdered at the hands of another was actually a murderer in a past life. The ripples in the pond of life are unpredictable. Control over our lives is an illusion.

If you feel you have further information to send about any of these cases, please send it to the e-mail address listed at the end of this book. If I feel compelled to do so, I will either contact you or forward it to the proper authorities.

Emma

1975 in the Pacific Region of the United States

It was a cool autumn morning as we donned heavy sweaters before going outdoors. Emma lived in a large white Victorian house on property that was mostly wooded. Her dog was well trained and waiting to go for a walk. My golden was just a pup and I struggled to settle her down before clipping the leash to her collar.

As we walked out the door, I looked back to see the screen door slam shut. I briefly wondered if the door was locked...and then turned my attention to the pulling dog at the end of my leash.

In this dream, I realized that I was the friend or rather, seeing through the friend's eyes. I felt tremendous guilt; both for not going inside to be sure the house was safe after our walk and at the feeling of relief that I didn't go inside.

Heavy feelings of remorse stung her friend for the simple fact that she is alive while Emma is dead. Emma was brutally murdered by an intruder who laid in wait for her in the house. She was attacked shortly after returning from her walk.

Kelly

1980 in the Northeast Region of the United States

We left the subway station together, with me following Kelly a few steps behind. It was her first time here. As she walked away from the station,

I began to realize that she didn't really have any particular destination in mind...she was just hungry.

Kelly had short bobbed golden brown hair and wore dark blue Jordache jeans with a fitted pink t-shirt. She carried a single gym bag slung over her shoulder. We didn't get very far before a man approached us. He was very interested in Kelly as he fell in step next to her.

He had done this before; dare I say he was practiced in this "predatory" behavior. I spoke up from behind them and said, "Don't talk to him, you don't know him." She turned her head to look at me and her expressive green eyes conveyed all that I needed to know. I sadly understood that she was no longer alive, a victim of this smooth-talking young man. I made a promise to her early in the morning of July 19th, 2010, to warn others to be more careful.

Liz

1983 in the Maryland/Washington D.C. Region of the United States

Liz did not spare me any suffering as I woke up at 1:15 AM on August 31, 2009 unable to breathe. She had been poisoned. She died slowly of respiratory failure, gradually enough to see and hear her killers arguing about her death and the missing information her department was responsible for reviewing.

Only Liz knew where it was located – and she never realized its' importance. I was with her and felt her panic and disbelief at the betrayal. With a low level security clearance at a government data processing office, she never thought she would be in harm's way. She was wrong. She went missing. Her body has never been found.

Chan Sook

1990 in the Pyongyang Region of North Korea

I'm sitting next to a manicured Korean woman who is definitely uncomfortable. We are meeting with someone of importance, someone who works behind the scenes as backroom deals are determined. He is a greasy, middle-aged man and I sense her complete repugnance.

He cannot see me as he suggests that she report a shady story about a government worker back to her agency. When she knows there is no proof for this false report, the woman is politely vague with her response. Moreover, it is understood that she will decline his entreaties.

He motions to the door and tells her to leave. She stands and bows while he remains seated and uninterested. He is already finished with her. She walks out the door, and as it shuts, she is taken. She is drugged and taken to a sanitarium. She dies from an incident with a fellow patient. Her young daughter never sees her mother again.

Tanya
1995 in the Southwest Region of the United States

I'm with Tanya, floating around her, as gunshots ring out. She looks left and right and grabs her children. She has an eight-year-old boy and ten-year-old girl. They are in a grocery store or military shopping center. She tells them to hide in-between aisles. They lie down and do not make any sounds. She knows there is a gunman very close. She can hear many more shots.

As she turns the corner, she sees several dead people lying in pools of their own blood. The shooter must be randomly killing people. At that moment of realization she sees the shooter and she is paralyzed with fear. He turns the corner of the aisle and aims his gun at her. She screams, "no"…but he doesn't care.

I look into his eyes; there is no anger, no hate and no remorse or feeling of any kind…they are just cold, hard and focused on destruction.

Anna
2010 in the country of Venezuela in South America

I am dreaming of a young girl with black hair and dark eyes. We are walking on a sunlit street, making our way into a great stone cathedral. We are holding hands and walking on the red carpeted center aisle. No one notices us. I realize at this point that we are at a funeral. We stand at the coffin and look at the person's body lying inside. It's her. She smiles at me, yet, she says nothing. We stand at the head of the cathedral, hand in hand, watching and listening to those around us.

The eulogy is being given by the priest. He is somber as he relates the details of her life. Her name is Anna and she is thirteen-years-old. Her death was violent at the hands of an eighteen-year-old young man. He was someone she had grown up with in the neighborhood and knew very well. It was a double loss for the community; a young girl was dead and a young man was on the run.

The girl's mother was wailing loudly and the family was in terrible distress. It was quite different with Anna. She was bright, happy and not concerned with the proceedings. She did not ask me to convey her anger or sadness. She did not ask me to help find her murderer. She was at peace.

I was confused at why I was present, why she had brought me to this place. After some consideration, I thought that perhaps my purpose was simply to witness her state of being, knowing that terrible circumstances can befall us and yet we can still maintain a happy and content disposition. Not everyone has needs following death. Some souls simply move on without any questions at all.

6

Assertion Of The Existence Of Non-Humans

Open Your Eyes and See

I have always been fascinated with books and movies about myths, monsters, creatures and beings from other worlds. If an angel existed, then why not a fairy or a unicorn, I reasoned. Moreover, if I could look up to the night sky and see other planets, stars and galaxies from here, then why couldn't beings from other planets look out and see us?

I was pleased when I met with a sleek, colorful mermaid in my dream one evening. I felt so free in a new world so full of wonder! How could this be Earth? It seems that there is always more to this world than what we can see…maybe all we have to do is to open our eyes and our minds in order to see that which usually remains hidden. Perhaps our world is much more wondrous than we think possible. How often are we quiet or still enough to look or listen for that which is not readily obvious?

I don't believe that the world holds secrets; I think that we see what we want to see and ignore anything that doesn't fit our idea of a world based in logic. Conceivably, it is we who remain a secret to ourselves.

The beings that chose to visit with me expressed no harmful intentions. Just the contrary, it seemed that they wanted to be understood and seen for what they are: unique and mortal. Every creature has a life span and every creature experiences death, even vampires.

Perhaps not all of the things we believe of these creatures are true, but there is at least a grain of truth to the idea of our beliefs in mythical creatures. The stories in this chapter will introduce some new ideas, concepts and opportunities to embrace a culture not entirely earth-like.

Danny

1865 in the Southeast Region of the United States

My dreams were dark and full of shadows on December 18th 2009. I smelled smoke hanging heavy around me. Gunshots cracked and the feral cries of men engaged in combat filled the air. As the din faded and smoke engulfed the battle, a new scene opened into a Civil War encampment.

A sandy blond-haired man approached me; he was seeking for assistance without speaking a word. His eyes betrayed an urgent need. He leaned close to me, speaking in hushed tones. He was desperate and afraid he would hurt his friends. He begged me to secretly help him as I was someone worthy of trust. The full moon was a day away, he said, and all had to be in order by then. Somehow, I already knew this.

His name was Danny and he was a shape-shifter – a Werewolf to be more exact. For some reason, I felt like I knew this and that it was a true fact. Incredibly, I knew I was a helper of sorts – a "safe" person. I'm not sure how I received this designation or from whom, but it was true and I knew what to do. I would make the proper arrangements.

Moments later, Danny introduced me to his much older brother, William. Surprisingly, I knew him already! It was then that I realized I was participating in Danny's recollection of an event that had already happened. I was seeing through the eyes of another, like being a stand-in for the real person.

I had some knowledge of this person and knew he held status at the camp. This person was in charge of camp set-up, and he was currently working on the location situation of the medical quarters. I greeted William warmly and shook his hand like he was an old friend...and then, of course, I realized that he was.

The following story was given to me by Danny over the course of about a week. It is told from his perspective.

Bare-Sarkers

I'm not sure how I got myself into this mess. I blame my father. He is a good man who, consequently, taught me how to be a good man. Be honorable in your actions. Be truthful. Respect yourself and the elders. Everything else will fall into place. Seems simple enough; we just tend to make things hard.

I want to explain a few things before we get started. I look to be a young man of eighteen, but I have said this for at least forty years. It is an effect of my genetics. I was born into Ulfhednar, the Wolf Clan, and I am a Were or shape-shifter. I had no control over this matter. The only control I have is how I deal with the associated responsibilities. I am blessed and cursed, as are we all.

My given name, Kveld, is of the old tradition. It means "twilight", for I walk in the place between dark and light. Light may be our preference, but darkness still descends in the natural order of the world.

As I have found, the light is always balanced with the dark, not because it wants to be, but because of necessity. At times, it may seem one has gained power over the other, however; the elders say if you take all of the good and all of the evil that is being wielded in this world, the outcome at the end of time will be complete balance. In effect, the two forces will cancel each other out.

For now, though, the fight between the two is ongoing and was set in motion at the beginning of time. One will never win over the other – it is the battle that matters, for in battle you discover the truth and all is laid bare.

My brother William is also a Were, however, he does not shape-shift. He looks to be much older than I, yet truly I am the elder by many years. I will still be here long after he has made his Journey, but I will watch over his children and their children. One day, I will have a son or maybe a grandson that will be like me and I will raise him as my father raised me. He will protect the survival of future generations of our lineage.

My father, who still keeps the old ways, is old for our kind; at least two hundred years old and probably getting ready to make his Journey. Sooner or later, he will simply leave and trek north to the Cold Lands. He will not return. It is a personal choice. He would not burden us with his age; he would choose to meet death on his own terms. It is honorable. He has lived long and well and I will miss him greatly. He has passed on the knowledge of our ancestors and taught me to live soundly in the present. Do not worry about the future. When the morrow comes, it will be the present and you will take some action; worry is nothing but a thief of present time.

It is a natural thing to wonder about your ancestors; many people consider from whence their bloodline originates. According to my father, our line is born from the blood of Vikings that migrated to North America from the Norselands around the year 1000 AD. Though they did not establish permanent settlements, many families chose to stay and move south when others returned to their homelands. My ancestors integrated further into the land, leaving the larger clan behind. The conquests were over. The wars had been fought. Our people were changing. The time to raise families had come...the time for peace. You may wonder why my ancestors chose to stay, but I know why and will tell you now the secret of my kind.

The men in my ancestral line belonged to a small group of elite warriors known as the Bare-Sarkers – known today as Berserkrs. This name actually means "no shirt" and refers to the common practice of going into battle without armor. Warriors would wear only the skin of a wolf or bear and would invoke Odinn, God of Fury and War, and go into battle protected and assisted by their animal totem.

They were fierce, possessed of phenomenal strength and were literally unconquerable. There was no fear for them, only complete and insatiable rage. They would strike down the enemy without any consideration during battle. It was surely a great and terrible sight. This altered state was bestowed upon them by Odinn, at their request, in order to ensure our survival as a clan.

Be advised that when one asks for help from the Gods, one must be willing to accept the answers given. It may not be the answer you expect and there may be unanticipated consequences. With everything, there is a payment to be made, for nothing is free. For us, the price is our sanity, logic and reason when in this state, as well as when the full moon is in the sky. This is Odinn's day and we pay homage no matter our will. It is a night of savage rage and fury. It is a night during which all responsible Were lock themselves away.

My ancestors would not begrudge Odinn his day on the full moon, yet, there was no reason any longer to make the Change at any other time. So, the ancestors began to set rules for the shape-shifters and started a partnership with humans in a secret society to help us when in need. They monitor us still today, as we allow it. Many times I have turned myself over to their care for the days before, during and after a Change, and I am always pleasantly surprised at the kindness provided me.

Now, to clarify the question you may be wondering about, there are two kinds of Were: those who shift consciousness and those that continue the Change physically with shape-shifting. They each live by different rules and both still walk the earth today. You may be one or know one and not even realize it until you've read my words.

Rage comes naturally to the offspring of Were lineage. At times, these people may snap into rage and not know from whence it comes. It is blinding. Something you would not normally do becomes a necessary action. It feels like someone else is taking over and you hold no power over them. A small and trifling situation may ignite quickly into a wildfire of fury. Some of this is genetic and some a build-up of unaddressed and misunderstood energy.

There is a lack of understanding about how to cleanse the body of the rage in a proper and regular manner. I feel sadness that many of you reading my words should have been taught, and yet, perhaps even your fathers did not know what they were. Take comfort in my words. Sometimes it only requires the recognition of your ancestors and the peace will come. At times, it may require the dedication of a regular time to address the energy.

Instead of being hurtful and aggressive towards others, find some activity where you can yell or hit. Sports are a natural option, as many sporting activities were born out of violent and competitive behaviors. The effect of ridding your body of this energy is mentally freeing and physically draining. It is a way to be responsible, achieve balance and still accept your status as a Were.

From time to time, a bare-sarker warrior would fall so naturally into a trance that he would continue to change...physically change into the animal he had chosen to share his soul with; the animal of his Clan. The Change was not usual.

These warriors were greatly respected and deeply feared. Their status suffered a low rank within the Clan for several reasons. One could avoid a warrior possessed in a trance and know them by their body dye and animal skins. One could not avoid a warrior gifted with the Change. That warrior had no presence of mind and all of the strength and fury of Odinn at his disposal. He was a creature that often killed loved ones and friends along with detested enemies. The Clan would never fully trust him. Thus, these warriors were often reviled and carried a great deal of guilt for their actions. They lived somewhat apart from the Clan.

As I stated earlier, my lineage is called Ulfhedinn or the Wolf Clan, and some of us have the ability to make the Change. Others are able to make the Bear Change, though I have not seen a Bjarn Clan member for many, many years. This could be because they have hidden themselves away in the deep forests or it could be that not many of them are left.

Pay attention to body types for they will be similar to Clan animals; you may recognize someone and they may not know themselves! Were genes may skip many generations and present suddenly. We believe that they are passed paternally, from father to son, though we cannot be sure. I have never seen or met a female Were, but that does not mean they do not exist; perhaps they keep themselves well concealed.

So far, I can tell you that I have never encountered a sorcerer, shaman or magic worker that could shape-change in the physical sense. I am not saying that they do not exist; I can only tell you my personal knowledge.

I know you are also wondering about the actual Shift. I can speak only of my experience and history. For most Were that I have met, it is as if they go from state of complete sobriety to utter seeming drunkenness within a matter of moments. That person's eyes may roll back in their sockets and head may loll as he is being filled with energy, overwhelming to his brain and heart to the point that he may fall down into a stupor or stagger around.

For those that continue the physical change, including myself, it proceeds with shivering and chills followed quickly by seeming fire coursing through my veins. Pain such as you can never imagine drops even the most seasoned Were to his knees. I always start to feel the cracking and popping just before a soft blackness creeps in…numbing my thoughts and pain until I am gone. There is no more thought until I return to myself again. I become the Wolf, not a hybrid being, as that would be monstrous indeed. I am in form of the wolf, both beautiful and terrible to behold as is our God, Odinn.

To the observer of either Change, one would notice the transformation spreading over the face of the person, and moreover, an alteration within the eyes; a distance or absence. Once this occurs, it is best not to be in the presence of that person...for they no longer know what they do and when they arise, the rage within them will consume them and control their actions. For Were, the hunting instinct combined with fury takes over. The hunt is for killing, not eating, and there is no preference for prey. There is no concept of mercy.

As I have stated before, there is no coherence in this state. While the fury lasts, Were are afraid of nothing. When the state is finally over, we are so powerless and feeble that it sometimes requires several days to recover. This is the time that we begin to remember what we have done...and the guilt soaks us to the bones if we have not taken proper precautions. It is enough to cause madness!

Please understand that many people do not believe in what they truly see or hear because it is too much for their minds to accept. Many choose to explain the unexplainable with logic. If you open your eyes to see, then you will see a world much greater than you ever thought possible.

Were exist. We live among you. We interact with you. We marry and have children with you. Just because you do not know something to be so, does not mean it is not so. Just because you do not understand something does not make it bad. Some people deem Were to be evil as told in so many stories, yet our roots are not in evil, but in survival. I have met many a human whom I knew was more evil than any Were I ever met.

The knowledge contained in this story is important and should not be lost; I realize not everyone has been as fortunate as I have been to know their history. So many of my kind do not know their origins, yet they know the pain of the Shift and know the freedom of power and power of guilt. It is important to know from whence you've come so that you can find your way and not repeat mistakes of the past.

{Danny's energy withdrew for a period of about three days, though he came back each night to make sure I would continue when he was ready. On the fourth night, he

continued with his story. I had the distinct feeling that for all of the extraordinary powerful energy he wielded, he felt quite helpless in the final day of his life.}

I stayed up too long…drank too much coffee. It's no use fighting the Change. I knew it was going to happen no matter how much coffee I drank. I suppose I was just trying to stay coherent and alert for as long as possible. I was nervous and pacing, locked in a well-built barn on a stranger's farm in the middle of nowhere. The arrangements had been made. It was not easy, but was the only responsible action I could take, the only safe way to go through the Change. Sometimes we have to do things that no one else understands, but it is the right action. At times, I believe that Fate intervenes and there is nothing that can change the outcome of an event and all that is left is the unfolding.

I could not have foreseen that my beloved Sarah was pregnant with our child. We had known each other only once and I considered her my mate. Though we were not married, we were of one soul. Human ways require much procedure and process. For us, much is decided by scent and attraction. We can smell strength and will be attracted, as well, we smell fear and know we can dominate. What I'm saying is that it is not about the paperwork, it is about real-time actions and agreements of instinct.

I could not know that I would not see her again. She had no understanding of why I sent her away. She was angry and did not want to go. She spoke her mind, paying no care to the adage that women should be silent unless asked to speak. She possessed a strong spirit. In my opinion, she was in fact and deed a true American woman. I liked that about her, but still did not allow her to remain. It was for her own safety.

I had noticed her from afar; sensed her will and character. I was drawn to her. I lured her to me. We knew we were matched for one another even though I had only courted her a fortnight. Thinking of her alone makes me miserable; nevertheless, she survived and lived a long and satisfying life without me and without ever marrying.

Alas, I think back to the many discussions I had with my father about war and fighting. He did not support my choice to fight with an army in war, as we were to have left that in the past. For us, violence can trigger the Change; it is very dangerous. He was being protective of his son, but there was wisdom in his words. I see that now.

I woke up two days after the battle. We had won. The Company had been systematically searching farms for the enemy that might be in hiding.

Soldiers, friends from my own company, found me in that barn hiding they thought. How could I explain what looked to be cowardly behavior?

Many of our friends had lost their lives in the fighting. Betrayal of your country was unforgivable. They were angry. They judged me harshly as a deserter and a coward. Words cannot adequately describe what happened, so I won't try. They did not wait for a trial; they simply hung me from the rafters of the barn. I had needed to recover, though they did not know it. I had not been able to fight or it would have been dangerous for them and for me. In the end, I should have understood that my place was not fighting in the front lines; I should have been fighting from my strengths – in silence and stealth.

I hold no ill will towards them. My only regret is that I was not able to meet my son, to raise him myself...for he is what I am or was... I have stayed this long stretch of time watching over him and my kin.

My brother taught him well. They named him Daniel, after me. Perhaps we will meet in a future life, as I go now to begin anew. Perhaps you will recognize my son one day; perhaps you will recognize me. Maybe you will see yourself a little bit clearer because of our story. I hope so. I have waited a long time for someone to listen and tell it. Fare thee well.

{Danny's energy departed quickly with no further words. It was as if there was a void...emptiness for me as his energy had been so focused and penetrating. I will miss him.}

Johnny

1965 in the country of Vietnam in Southeast Asia

The dream is a muddle of green and brown in the beginning. I can feel a steady muffled beat hitting the air around me. The picture comes into focus, crystallizing in its clarity and I get a rush of adrenaline. I'm in the open doorway of a large green helicopter flying low over brown, murky water. It is tropical-hot; the humidity is so high that I can hardly breathe. I feel the sweat trickling down my face and middle of my back.

Crouching low, I look out the open door and see another helicopter drop out of the air...black smoke trailing. It hits the water. I can't hear anything because everything is too loud and I realize that it's from the gunfire and missiles exploding all around. I'm filled with intense hate; it's an extreme immensity in my chest and numbness in my head. I want to kill the enemy because those are my friends that just went down.

"Take us lower," I shout with a downward wave of my hand. I do not recognize it as my hand as it is a man's hand. I am actively participating in this dream, yet I am fully aware that I am with someone, sharing their thoughts. We jump and we're out of the helicopter and into the water.

Time slows and I can see each blade of the Huey flash overhead. It rises like a great lumbering dragon into the air and flies away. Gunfire cracks close by. It's time to move, but we're just a little too late. Searing pain radiates throughout my left shoulder. Blood flows from the wound creating a blooming red stain, but we make it to the riverbank. We start to feel lightheaded when another blast of pain sears through our right leg. We go down. Our vision blurred with pain, mixing the green of the jungle, the red of blood and the fusion of the two as a deluge of rain poured out on us all.

Thus my journey began with Johnny. Johnny possessed a very persuasive energy and the information contained herein has the potential to help you understand yourself and the people around you better. Present time is November 9, 2010.

Knowledge is Power

I woke up in a dark, muddy cell as a prisoner of war. I was alone. My wounds had not been addressed. My captors were nowhere to be seen. I stayed quiet. I'm not sure how long I laid there, propped up against a wall made of cracked mud and straw, but it felt like forever. It gave me a lot of time to think.

{We did not look back at his exact thoughts as they were dark and full of questions. He felt worse after giving time and energy to those thoughts and would have done well to move forward instead of looking back at 'what if' and 'could have/should have' scenarios. He has made it clear that the purpose of this story is not about his time as a POW; moreover, it is about survival, acknowledgement and awareness. He is not plagued with feelings of revenge or hatred. He learned from this terrible experience and would like to empower you with this knowledge.}

When my captors came for me the first time, it was to look at my wounds. My leg wound was shot through and through, so even though it had bled a lot, it was not life-threatening. I was worth more to them alive than dead, so they cleaned and dressed it. My shoulder, in contrast, was a mess. There was something definitely broken and the shrapnel had to be pulled out. I have never felt more excruciating pain in my entire life. There was no anesthesia; they just held me down and did what needed to be done. Thankfully, I blacked out several times during this ordeal and finally woke up back in my little cell…alone again in the dark.

The next few weeks I saw very little food or water. My shoulder ached constantly but wasn't infected as far as I could tell. I had no fever. My only companions were the rats, cockroaches and things that crawled in the dark. I was glad many times that I could not see what was moving around.

A kind of delirium began to take over. Perhaps it was the lack of light and companionship with the constant pain. It became as if I had fallen from space and time into a black hole of nothingness. Strangely, it was a glad change from the disgusting cell in which I was actually living. I felt it happening, the losing of my mind, my sane mind trying so hard to make sense of things that made no sense at all.

In time, in the darkness, I began to see wisps of light in many different colors. At times I would try to touch them and other times I would deny their existence, thinking I had finally gone crazy.

One day, after a week of no food, the light wisps became more rounded and solid. I was so weak; I wanted to eat anything. I grabbed at a particularly bright light and I saw something incredible. Though I had touched nothing, the light began to move to my hand. The moment that it happened, I felt better – yet the original light dimmed slightly. It didn't take very long, just a moment, and I was able to sleep for a few minutes and gain some true rest.

I tried this again and again and each time I was able to achieve the same result. I began to routinely take light from the things that were creeping in my cell…though I never killed anything; I was able to sense when I was hurting something. My captivity became easier to contend with and my body began to heal. I was still in a constant state of hunger and thirst, nonetheless I was able to survive long enough that my captors eventually moved me to a pit where I could see the sun and sky at times, and more importantly, there were people around.

I had learned. I began to view my captors in a different way. What made them different from the creeping things in my old cell? Nothing. Everything holds some kind of light. People held light just the same. I began to watch them when they came near. I noted how they looked and acted and with my newly changed way to look at things, I was able to shift my vision to see the glow that surrounded them. They became my targets.

After a time, I didn't even need to be near them in order to feed from their light. I pictured each guard in my mind. I imagined drawing their energy from them, specifically watching it flow into me as a bright stream of light. I was able to feel the energy revitalizing me, healing my shoulder, making me feel less hungry and thirsty. I drew it all into myself and felt satisfied and never once guilty.

I saw the immediate effect I was having on them. Sickness and fear spread throughout the camp as I could see changes in the light that I now know as the "Aura" of those I had attacked...and I systematically weakened them and grew stronger daily. My body looked thin, but I was strong and able to move easily and think clearly.

The day that I was rescued, the soldier that helped me from my hole said that I had the clearest eyes he had ever seen, especially for a sick, mal-nourished and wounded POW. I had been in captivity for seven months. I had changed in many ways; ways I could never have foreseen.

What's important for you to know is that not all people are good people...many are ignorant and many are easily fooled. The majority of people sleepwalk through life and become victims without even knowing it. There is a world that most people never see; a world that most do not believe even exists. There is a world of light energy. Be aware. Stop, look and listen to what is happening to you and around you. Look at your life from a whole different perspective, at the events and people with whom you choose to surround yourself and that choose to surround you. How do you feel when you are around certain people or even when you think about certain people? Trust your instincts.

Think about it this way...blood is life. It is a mystery that flows through our veins providing everything we need; even rudimentary creatures and insects have some sort of blood. It contains energy. Everything is energy; all that we do is exchange it from one form to another. Energy is life...and I took it greedily whenever I could when I was in captivity. I did not know it at that time, but I was a natural energy vampire. When my life was threatened, my innate ability surfaced in a way that I could acknowledge it.

In fact, when I think about it, I had always been able to get what I wanted...I just didn't know how it happened. Force of will made things happen for me. I possessed a will that was so strong with energy that it ruthlessly sought out any ways and means to make what I wanted to happen to occur and it caused it to occur. I now know that energy transfer takes many forms. Because I am aware, I have responsibility to manage it without hurting anyone.

There are those who take energy that know what they are doing and there are those that do not know what they are doing. Energy vampires who are aware will deliberately take energy from others, usually by instinctive ability, bolstered by practice. Most will choose to take energy directly from their prey's aura.

Energy vampires that are unaware do not understand what they are and tend to make their way through life without fully understanding how they are achieving or maintaining health or success. They may or may not be cognizant of the effect they have on others, although they can see the results. Energy vampires tend to have a difficult time maintaining relationships of any kind until they understand their affect on others and how to exercise some control. They tend to seem somewhat emotionally unstable to others, swinging from high to low quickly. Most have a magnetic quality to their personality, attracting others easily.

I want you to know that energy exchange is a most natural and wonderful phenomenon. Everything and everyone in the world participates in this activity, but most do not recognize it for what it is. For example, I love to take hot showers when I am feeling sick, sad or depressed. I never understood why until I really thought about it. The water holds heat. When I stepped into the shower, I began to absorb the heat in an energy exchange. My body and aura absorbed the heat and replenished my depleted stores of energy. This is a simple example, but note that nothing is harmed.

When nature is involved, nothing is harmed. Keep in mind that when positive feelings like love or happiness are exchanged, then both the giver and receiver are energized. The true challenge is achieving recognition of energy exchange and maintaining balance.

You should know that those energy vampires that are unaware are not consciously trying to hurt you, but they do anyway. Watch for those people who always consider themselves the victim. You do not need to listen to every horrible thing that happened to them; this takes away from your happiness and allows them to absorb your energy. You do not have time to listen to them whine; give them your honest opinion if they ask it (which will probably displease them) and then stop listening. Put up an energy shield and protect yourself. They will lose interest quickly when they don't get the response from you that they want. They will find someone else to prey upon.

Think also about people who constantly criticize you and make you feel guilty for the choices you have made; you are in charge of your own life just as they are responsible for their own life. You do not need to take their criticism to heart. It takes away your self-confidence and bolsters their attacks on you. You feel worse when it is all finished and they feel better somehow. Stop the cycle.

How about the person who is always caught up in something too dramatic to believe? They want to tell you about the terribly bad situation and maybe get your advice, but somehow they do most of the talking and it wears you out; nothing you say has an effect on how they feel, nor do they change how they will deal with the situation. This is because the point of telling you is to lull you into a state of mind that is easy to draw energy from.

If you feel unduly burdened as this is happening, it is because they are unburdening themselves on you; taking your energy and leaving you with negativity to ponder. Chances are that they have held this same conversation with several other people that day, week, month or longer if it is something they can resurrect in order to evoke certain marker feelings and you are just the next person on their list. Each time they tell their story, they get better at honing it and expect certain response feelings or comments from you. They are not listening. It is a waste of your time. Do not be a victim.

Finally, there is the person who always has to be the center of attention. This person is always talking over others and never allowing anyone else to enjoy the flow of energy (attention) from another person or group. This person does not want to share any attention and needs all of the energy or focus from the group in order to feel okay.

This is the kind of person that gets very depressed when they are alone; they are constantly seeking somewhere to go or something to do and usually with as many people involved as possible. People such as this will have their "regulars" who will go along with them. These people will follow their leader because they feel the connection; they do not realize they are the sheep following the wolf. These people show addictive behavior traits; oftentimes, cult leaders and adrenaline junkies would fall into this category...or it could be as simple as your loud spoken neighbor next door who attends home owner association meetings drawing attention to minor issues.

For another example, let's say that you have a fight with your friend and you can't stop thinking about the fight, maybe how unfair or unreasonable you think they are being or how much you wish you could take something back that you said. By dwelling in this state of mind, you are choosing to disperse your energy to a situation that cannot be helped. Cut it off. Literally, cut it off. Picture a pair of scissors fit to do the job and clip the cords of energy running to that person or situation. You will immediately feel better. There is only here and now. Deal with situations as they happen or when you are next with that person.

Leave the past in the past and do not allow your energy to seep from you; it's like a small cut that bleeds just a little...one cut isn't so bad, but with many cuts a person can die from blood loss, though it may be a slow, painful process. Look at your energy exchanges and know that they continue to happen even though people leave our presence.

If you are going to be a responsible person in this life, you must also think about yourself and how you affect other people. It is almost impossible for some of us to realize the incredible power we hold over others; the power of our words, emotions and moods. Whether you realize it or not, you carry this energy within your aura, which can expand instantly to encase another person or an entire building! Be aware of what energy you produce and take. Maybe you are an energy vampire! The good news is that you can learn to control yourself.

People who are sensitive to energy can sometimes feel overwhelmed in social gatherings or crowds. There is so much energy moving around, and it is all different, that one who is sensitive to energy that is unaware will simply absorb everything to the point that they will need to withdraw and be alone for awhile. They can actually experience physical symptoms of sickness in the presence of sick people.

Energy vampires can empathically feel other people's emotions, sometimes experiencing them as their own. When others are happy around them, they may feel elated and vigorous...though the effects on those happy people being fed upon (consciously or unconsciously) can be sudden depression or fatigue. Normally happy and positive people will learn to avoid energy vampires; it is a natural defense of which they are probably not even aware. An energy attack is an uninvited and unwelcome taking of a person's vital energy. This is what I did when I was captured; though I feel it was acceptable given the circumstances. I did not do this when I returned home. An attack can happen through casual contact, from a distance or even through dreams. Please understand that many people will use whatever means they can in order to satisfy their needs and desires. Some people will take joy in your fears, going so far as to exploit your fears in dreams, for this creates more energy for them to feed upon.

I often attacked my captors in this way and many of them, I could tell, felt an aversion toward me though I'm not sure they knew why. I would never suggest trying to hurt anyone, all the same, I tell you so that you will be able to tell if you are being attacked.

Conscious attacks can include mind and or dream manipulation, causing the victim to hear, see, and feel things. Attacks of this nature can range from mild to very severe, sometimes leaving the victim depressed or even physically sick.

If you wake up from a nightmare, clear your home with white light energy by envisioning your home filled with bright light. Darkness cannot stay where there is light. You can protect yourself. Envision yourself surrounded by an invisible force field that deflects unwanted or negative energy. If you feel suddenly drained, consciously repel the negative energy; see it in your mind as bouncing off of the force field surrounding you. I sometimes send it back to the source from whence it came.

Most energy vampires get greatly invigorated as feeding can cause a drug-like rush. Therefore, it should be no surprise that energy feeding can be very addictive. Energy vampires feel that they must have the energy they require on a regular basis and will experience discomfort if they are denied access to a source. Symptoms of "energy deprivation" for an energy vampire are much the same as for an addict and can include extreme fatigue, depression and emotional behavior with acute highs and lows. Recognize this and do not be a victim.

Finally, it may seem hard to comprehend, but energy vampirism can present in a self-contained, parasitic form that turns inward to feed upon oneself. In this way, the person paradoxically becomes both vampire and victim. Phobias, obsessions, and compulsions are all examples of feeding upon oneself. In many cases, people who suffer from these conditions have a past history from a previous lifetime that presents in their current life-time. Inexplicably, people can be instantly restored when they become aware through the knowledge presented in this text.

Knowledge remains perhaps the most powerful force in the universe. One of humanity's greatest challenges is discovering knowledge and apply-ing it to empower us while making the world a better place for all.

When it came close to the time for me to die, I verily willed my soul to leave my body. I did not suffer and languish with the decision. Remember that death does not hold any power over you.

Zoe

1970 in the Great Lakes Region of the United States

I fell into a deep and peaceful sleep on the evening of May 17, 2010. I felt happy to be enclosed in the deep blue darkness. When I opened my eyes in the dream, it was a beautiful sunlit day, though the sun shone in rays dancing about the sand at my feet. Then I realized I had no feet; I saw fins! My body was covered in gorgeous translucent scale-like skin. It looked to be reflective and yet absorptive of the colors around me, blending beautifully with the water and making me all but invisible.

I felt along my torso...it was so smooth...and then looked at my slightly webbed hands. At the end of each finger was a dangerous claw-like fingernail. Of course, I was underwater. I didn't want to breathe, but once I tried, I was incredulous that I could! It was then that I sensed a pres-ence...someone giggling in the background of my mind...at my shock of breathing under water. I was not alone; I shared this body with another. In fact, she had called me to this place so that I might experience the wonder of her world.

Her name is Zoe. She has felt that some of the true wonder of our world has been forgotten. Scientists know nothing but a tiny bit about our world; they are just beginning to make true discoveries. It is sad that they often feel if something cannot be seen, then it does not exist. One cannot see air, Zoe noted, and yet you know it is there because you breathe it, you notice the lack of it when you are under water. Her point being that just because no one has proven the existence of mermaids doesn't mean they, and other creatures like them, do not exist.

Zoe seemed sad that the fishermen no longer pay homage to her kind. The myths of the kindness and ferociousness of the mer-people are no longer told. A-tala, as she calls it, (Atlantis) is long gone and I can tell that she laments the loss of that culture. I felt her repugnance at the ignorance at some of the practices and baseness of our own current world culture. She wonders if we have lost our sense of what is right and what is wrong. Have we forgotten that which is truly beautiful?

She is mesmerized by her surroundings even though it is familiar and home. She laughs and spins, churning the sand on the ocean floor. I feel elated as we rocket and glide through the water. It is what I think a dolphin must feel as he swims so playfully and effortlessly.

The water is cool and peaceful, yet not as quiet as you might expect. There were so many sounds; clicking and clacking, banging and swishing…I had always thought it would be a silent place. It is a place alive with sound and activity with currents always pushing and pulling. This place is surreal, magical and in some ways, frightening.

Zoe is telepathic and the following is what she chose to share.

A Suitable Place to Live

It would be difficult for a human to pronounce my real name, so you may call me Zoe, which is similar. I want to talk to you about many things, but mostly about the places we live. This includes our bodies, our homes and even the planet or solar system we inhabit. It is time that a new understanding of choice is realized.

I would like for you to strongly consider the idea of reincarnation. To expect to learn all that we need to know in one lifetime does not make any sense. We are not perfect. Truly we need many, many lifetimes in order to figure out even simple things. Of course, we are all unique and learn at different paces. I am an old soul and will most likely stop incarnating soon. My people, the ones I began incarnating with, are almost gone now, having learned that which they needed in order to leave the physical world and begin with new spiritual responsibilities. New souls are constantly being born and this new crop of souls are slowly replacing us. Some of the tenacious old ones, perhaps like me, will stay to shepherd them along for awhile.

Souls are created from the Source. Imagine a place of great light and happiness with many guides working with the essence of the Divine

Source- extracting and caring for the very souls that populate the planets. The Guides do not control what a soul is or is not; they only accept what the Source allows as a soul and then nurtures and teaches it. We are not inherently male or female; we are each unique. There is no one exactly like you anywhere in any universe. With an open mind, consider that we are all suited to different kinds of life; aquatic, arboreal, land-dwellers and many others you can't imagine for we are NOT all the same.

There are innumerous planets on which we can manifest our souls. Our higher guides, in their infinite wisdom, choose the most suitable planets for us on which to incarnate and choose the most suitable and ready species with whom to share a body. Planets are constantly being born, thriving and dying such as we do, just on a grander and slower scale.

That is what happened to my home planet...a sun in our solar system collapsed and therefore, my planet died. I am not from Earth, yet this planet is sufficient and beautiful in its own right. The Advanced Ones monitor all of the planetary shifts with the knowledge that nothing stays the same and everything changes. Everything is constantly changing though you do not recognize it as the changes are so minute. We tend to notice the accumulation of change.

I survived on this planet, in the same body, for three centuries. I chose this body with my guide while still on the Other Side. I had several candidate bodies to choose from but it was in this particular body that I felt I would learn the most. I felt a connection with it more than the others that were available to me.

No one can know for sure how good the bond will be between body and soul, but I do know that there are times when souls choose bodies that do not match or connect well. Sometimes this is undertaken in order to learn or experience something new and other times it is driven by the talent or beauty that a particular body possesses.

By the same token, sometimes souls will try to live in other worlds than the one chosen for them by their guides. This can be an extremely difficult transition, leading to awkwardness, imbalance and sometimes depression or not belonging. Oftentimes the soul who does this has dreams of strange places and creatures that do not exist on Earth. If you feel this way, reach out to the stars and ask from whence you came – perhaps you will get the answer and feel some connection and comfort at the challenge you have undertaken.

At times, many people feel that they are constantly fighting their bodies. The answer is to ask "why". Talk to your body, it will listen and reply. You will be very surprised at your ability to connect and correct some of the issues with which you have been plagued. Treat your body like a child, giving it what it needs but not always what it wants. It does not always know what is best for it.

Your soul is much logically smarter than your body. At the same time, listen to what your body tells you; it speaks to you in the only language it knows: the physical language. Eat when you are hungry, sleep when you are tired, exercise when you are restless; this is very simply how to keep your physical balance. Moderation in all is key.

To continue with my story, I crossed over from the physical world into the spiritual world where I am now as an elder of great age. I was responsible for the re-telling of the ancient tales. We do have a written culture, but our stories are kept and told from one generation to the next. I wish to tell you something of our culture and heritage, for it is mixed with yours.

A-tala was the name of a great white marble city of tall columned structures and immense temples. It was on an island in a most beautiful area of the calm and warm aqua-blue ocean. It was an ancient city by the time disaster struck. A-tala was swallowed by the sea due to the shaking of the earth and huge waves during a terrible lightning storm. Fireballs fell from the sky and destroyed much of the once gorgeous city.

The City was lost to world of man, but the opportunity was seized by the Advanced Ones. When my planet was lost, Earth, and more specifically, A-tala was chosen as our new home. We merged our souls with the bodies of the creatures that already inhabited this planet's oceans – for if you are not aware, many planets are seeded with DNA just for this reason… similar DNA means an easier time re-establishing contact and connection.

It is a mutually beneficial relationship. Body and soul come together in order to help one another; each lends their heightened senses in order to protect, feed and procreate as well as being comforted by the presence of the other. You are a merger of two, which is why at times, you feel pulled in different directions. However, the soul is infinitely stronger than the body.

A-tala was reborn under the ocean waves. It is located now in very deep water at the bottom of a large fissure. It is not cold as there are lava fields nearby of which we take advantage– it's beautiful, really, watching the creation of the world. This same creative force that builds the Earth also destroys it…it is a familiar cycle and the correct way of things. The old is destroyed and the new is reborn. I miss the planet that I called home for so many lifetimes; nevertheless, I do feel that this is my home now.

From a distance, A-tala glows many shades of pink, green and yellow, though it is sheltered from above by the towering walls of the fissure. The lights are of a phosphorescent nature; living lights that are protected and cared for by our denizens.

My ancestors claimed the ruins of A-tala and rebuilt them with the many treasures that the ocean has claimed and still collects. It is richly decorated with fine statues, jewels, gold and silver; yet, just as beautiful are the corals and sea fans that choose randomly where to live. It is a living city; calm and settled.

Unfortunately, there are many natural dangers present here. We still fall prey to the sharks and other monsters of the sea. Vigilance is always necessary. We protect ourselves with weapons and post guardians that keep us safe. Humans please note here that you should also be vigilant and walk the Earth with open eyes; predators stalk the land still, though you may not readily recognize them as such. If something doesn't feel right, then it probably isn't. Beware.

Mer-people are a peaceful race and do not like conflict. Our society is mostly crime free; however, being telepathic creates some temptation for a few of our kind. It is a terrible crime to invade someone's mind or thoughts. Unfortunately, some unscrupulous yet gifted humans are now discovering how to do this and there is no way for anyone to catch them; telepathic connection is routinely dismissed as impossible in the human world. Please be aware that telepathy is possible in the human world and is the only way that my kind communicates.

We have only experienced a few instances of mind rape, which is what we call this crime, in my lifetime; it is a serious offense that is dealt with swiftly. Perpetrators' telepathic connection to the group is severed permanently. These criminals are never fully able to redeem themselves for this crime is seen as a sickness for which there is no cure. Though we do not ostracize them, we take care and do not leave opportunities for them to trespass. It is a very sad circumstance, but necessary precaution.

On the Other Side, if a soul has committed crimes in his or her previous lifetime, there is the need and requirement to review and discuss their actions with their guide and the Council. At times, a soul may believe themselves to be too damaged to return and properly function and ask to go through a cleansing program. This is not to be taken lightly. This kind of program is the reorganization and restructuring of a soul at the Source level; it effectively changes the essence of that soul so that it will not be the same as it was once. The cleansing program is never imposed on any soul; it is undertaken by choice.

If a soul believes that there is no hope and has taken counsel or advice with no change in their behavior, then they are left to consider the karmic ramifications they have created. If they do not feel they can change and that they will hurt others in future lifetimes, the choice to be broken down into basic light particles returning to the Source is offered to them. A long period of isolation from the Group and guidance with Advanced Guides precedes any action of Soul Disbandment. I do not know how many times this has occurred, however; I know it is not often. It is the true death of an individual soul; it is karmic balance reinstatement. The journey is ended and eventually restarted as part of another formed soul. There is always hope for us; nonetheless, the energy of our actions always returns to us and we must come back into balance.

A-tala was once a grand and busy city above the ocean and now rests as a muted city below the waves. There is balance in this development. It is an arrangement of outer turbulence leading to inner peace. Though a great catastrophe befell the City, a vast serenity now pervades its streets. It is like this with living creatures as well.

Some of you may still dream of that City...maybe in short sequences, for it was so long ago that you incarnated there. Truly we all come from the same Source and we are all on a journey returning to the same Source. Our journeys, each one, enriches the Source; along the way, we enhance and enjoy one another's personal experiences. Each of us contributes to the knowledge, development and ever-changing, all-knowing Source of All That Is.

I have chosen, through the telling of this story, to return once again to Earth; this time as a human! I feel challenged and yet, I must know what it is like to live above the waves and walk on legs. I want to bring my rich culture and heritage to you, to share information about telepathy and communication. I feel this is my next great adventure. I hope my guide will agree! Until I find my land legs, I bid you farewell.

Red Planet

In my dream, I felt the crossing from the normal dream-state into another state of new dimension. I have traveled far into the future. I have become a visitor on another planet; a red, rocky place…a place that humans "seeded" with "pilgrims" long ago. Earth, in this time, has been gone for quite some time. I am not sure how I know this except that the knowledge was simply there.

Future Survival

It was as if I had arrived through a portal; inter-dimensional travel was now known and regulated, but still unusual. I was standing outside on what I would consider a small landing pad. The atmosphere was breathable though there was a slightly metallic smell in the air. There was absolutely no wind that I could feel. The sky was pale green with no clouds in sight.

I saw, standing near me, a wrinkled creature that I knew to be an alien life form. He was very short and exhibited light yellowish-grey skin that seemed very dry. He communicated with me without speaking, not because he couldn't, but because he chose telepathy as a way that would not cause me undue shock at his voice. I knew that he had been steward to visitors, such as me, for many human generations. His kind lives many lifetimes to that of humans and he is well over 200-years-old.

The alien was waiting for me; he motioned which way we were to go. He led me to a middle-aged man with brown hair and dark eyes. He sported a well-trimmed beard and looked ruggedly handsome in my opinion. He was so happy to see me and I was not privy as to the reason why. No matter. He hugged me and took my hand. No words had yet escaped my lips or his.

The creature summarized that the man was a pilot and wanted to show me his ship. The man seemed eager to show me many advances that had been made since my time. The alien, me and the man embarked his ship. It was a small vessel, oval in shape with a door that formed and dissipated just as quickly as one could walk through it. There was nothing inside the ship except three free standing chairs and a few lighted panels.

We sat in the chairs that looked like soft silver eggs located in the center of the craft. The chairs seemingly melted and conformed completely to our bodies; every part was supported with an extremely soft fluid-like form of memory foam. Though we had no seat belts, when we lifted off, it was the most wonderful feeling…and so fast! The chairs were stable, but the part we sat in, moved like a floating compass, no matter the maneuvering, we were secure and upright in our seats. It was like I was riding the smoothest, fastest roller coaster imaginable, but it was incredibly comfortable and not frightening at all. We had a full screen view of the outside as the interior wall of ship had all but disappeared and we were ostensibly outside and not in the ship at all!

The man showed me how he could maneuver the ship; he could even take us into and through the red rock of the planet with no damage to his ship.

The alien signaled to the man who then changed his excited and happy demeanor to something more serious, turning the ship on a course to an unknown destination. We docked the ship and walked from the landing pad high on a red rock cliff through a large rough cave opening. We walked a bit further into the cave and through some clear doors fixed in the rock of a smaller cave opening. I know these were not glass but some material that was much stronger. We walked more deeply into the smaller cave and we came to a highly carved and stylized rock archway. We entered what seemed to be his home. The entire room was carved from the beautiful banded red rock.

A young woman came into the room with a baby. She did not pause on her way to me. I couldn't help noticing her odd beauty. She wore robes of a warm yellow that accentuated her slender form. Her hair was long and dark, but it was more than that; she simply glowed with health. The man was her husband and she was the mistress of the house. I did not know her, except when I saw her blue eyes I recognized them as my own, like my mother's eyes, like her mother's eyes. She smiled what seemed to me a knowing smile. She was quietly proud.

She gave the baby over to me and I was so pleased to be trusted to hold her. Then, the man placed his hand on my forearm and I knew that my line would not die out. Here in front of me were my distant future line. At a time in history, many women took their husband's names and followed the paternal line; not in that future time. It was a maternal society and I was allowed to know that I was that young woman's ancestor. I was holding the continuation of my lineage, a baby girl, and his daughter. There was no animosity at the birth of a girl. Women had become, once again, the acknowledged givers of life.

I have no sons in my current life, though I had wanted a son in order to appease my parents as they had no sons. When I did become pregnant, I gave birth to a healthy, beautiful daughter. I was so happy at her arrival, yet I felt anger and sadness at her father's disappointment that our child was a girl.

I will have no further children in this lifetime. I have struggled with the thought that my father's lineage would not continue, however, I was reminded that in some cultures, proper lineage follows though women. I am blessed. I am satisfied. I no longer wonder about the future of my lineage, but also of the future of the human race. We are survivors. We will survive.

I am told that I was allowed this visit in order to set my mind at ease as well as to inform others who may read this story to know that they have the ability to ask their own questions and get answers. The way is now open. If you want to know of your future, you have only to ask. Open your mind, dream, meditate, listen to music – do whatever it is that helps you to relax – and then be prepared to listen for the answers.

7

Advice From Advanced Souls

Be Bold and Speak

At times, it is fine and good to quietly work behind the scenes for change as it may be the best way to make a difference in this world. However, there always comes a time when this approach is not enough. As you will see from the stories in this part of the book, sometimes decisive action must be taken. A stand must be made for those ideals in which you believe.

As we look through times past, it is easy to see patterns of thought and behaviors that were unhealthy for humanity. We can see the progress made from then until now because some person thought that a change needed to be made. The people who changed those outmoded ways of thinking were just average citizens who decided that something needed to be changed.

A small idea presented in the proper way can gain traction very quickly in some segments of the population. When a person takes a stand on some issue, that individual puts themselves in the way of criticism; the world does not lack for critics, but for leaders. Leaders become the target for anger because new ideas put people in an uncomfortable state of possible change. Many people choose ignorance instead of education on a matter and will therefore not understand what is trying to be accomplished.

Sometimes, our convictions come at great personal cost. Friends and family will not always understand or support your principles. Even though it feels right in your heart, when you are under fire, you may question if you are doing the right thing. Do not measure yourself by others or their opinions. If you are working from your heart with a clear attitude and good intentions then you should follow what you know to be right.

You may never know how you affect those around you because the only ones who you will ever hear from are those who love or hate what you have to say. There are so many others that will say nothing at all. Those people are the ones who may take time to think about what you have said, watch your actions and carefully consider your idea.

If one of those people truly thinks about what you have said and then reconsiders how they feel and even possibly makes a change...then you have done what you were called to do. We do not have the luxury of defining what constitutes success. Change starts with one person and continues on from that person to many others and so on. This is how our societal values and mores shift. It is unfortunate that many times ignorance rules the masses and we must contend with mob mentality.

One of the best ways to create change is by introducing a new way of thought. As you will see, this can be a painful and difficult process. It starts, as always, with a vision and a person to champion that ideal. The resistance to new ideas can be very great. You must realize that you cannot argue with ignorance or anger. Illogical people do not speak from a rational state of mind, nor do they want to hear logic from you. Most people are comfortable in their own space with their normal patterns. Ingrained patterns are difficult to change.

Oftentimes, even if what you are introducing is something good and will improve lives, people will fight the change because it is different than what they know. They do not want to know the new information because then it is required for them to actually think and form new opinions and change their behaviors accordingly; this can be daunting and very scary.

Follow what you know to be right even though others may not understand or agree with you. You were put here to make a difference; sometimes that simply means asking the questions that force others to think.

Aloysius

1745 in the Ile-de-France Region of France

Frère Jacques, Frère Jacques,	Are you sleeping? Are you sleeping?
Dormez-vous? Dormez-vous?	Brother John, Brother John?
Sonnez les matines!	Morning bells are ringing!
Sonnez les matines!	Morning bells are ringing!
Din, dan, don. Din, dan, don.	Ding, dong, ding. Ding, dong, ding.

Aloysius came to me first as a slight dark-haired child of about nine years old. He quite unabashedly sang a child's song to me...Frère Jacques... in French! Then giggling, he ran away and his voice became but an echo in my dream. Perhaps there is a double meaning to this song.

My dream darkened and morphed to take on a more serious tone. I knew I was in Paris. I stood on a very small island in the middle of a slow moving river. I knew this scene had happened many years ago – sometime in the 1700's, even though for me, it was September 13, 2008.

Fire crackled near to me and acrid smoke filled the air. As I looked around, I instinctively backed away. I was sickened to see that two men had been lashed together back to back on their knees. They were blackened and burning in a smoldering fire; I was saved from seeing them suffer as they were already dead and unrecognizable. An adult Aloysius spoke to me with a thick French accent, "Quaere Verum."

Thus began his story and truly I understood that he carried with him the burning of that fire in nightmares of his own. I have tried to relate all that he wanted to say in the following stories told as much as possible with his own words.

Seek the Truth

I am not Frère Jacques that the song names. That song was sung, then as it is now, about my dear friend Jacques de Molay. A great man to be sure. A great man in battle, level-headed and respected; hard broken in torture, but broken nonetheless...as were we all.

As the hour grows late and I lay my head upon the pillow, the nightmares begin. I often awake in a terrible sweat...there is no relief from the heat...and when I look down to my legs and feet, I see blackened skin and bones. The torturous burning is not a quick death, it is hours long and agonizing as I smell my own flesh cooking. We did no wrong, unless serving

God and Country is wrong...of that we are guilty...and they murdered us for it.

My name in that life was Geoffroy de Charney, and I was Grand Preceptor of Normandy, a respected governor. I know this because I have dreamt it. I was brought into the Templar Order by my brother. I took vows of chastity, poverty, and obedience. I was only sixteen, yet I was considered a man. I knew of bravery, strength and honor and was most willing to protect pilgrims and fight off savage hordes that threatened their travels to the Holy Land.

I assure you that I lived the life worthy of the most powerful order of military monks known as the Knights Templar. I was strong. We, as a people, were strong... but now you and your people have forgotten the truth of everything. It will not come to you easily as someone laying out for you upon a silver platter. This is not the way of things. You must seek out the truth, every day and not in passing.

I was murdered in that life and chose to be reborn in another body, and yes, I know I am now dead, just very stubborn. I am very pleased that someone took the time to finally listen to me and write down my words for they are important and you are ready to hear them.

In my most recent life I was a priest and schoolmaster plagued with terrible nightmares. Instead of asking why, I buried myself in work and prayer. The burning never left me and it was only after I died that I recalled what had happened. Yes, trauma can follow you from one life to another, however; you can and should address it. Don't let it continue to bother you. Talk to your pain and you may be surprised at the answers you receive as you dream.

I became a progressive teacher with many new ideas and methods. I kept myself busy writing books and teaching. I was obsessed. I sought no rest of writing books and I wrote too many to count. I believe the only true way our world changes is through our children. It is time to teach our children right ways. We have lost generations to ignorance and self serving behavior...will we ever recover? What has happened to chivalry and protection of those who require it?

I seek peace through a message of change to the living. I will speak to you various truths and yet many of you will see me as a heretic. Be assured, I do not seek your acceptance, only to show you the way to the truth. This will give me the peace that I need in order to return to the earthly world instead of simply watching and waiting.

I speak now at too much length for I have a story to tell. It begins thus, at the beginning.

Phillip the Fair

I am sure that you have heard of the Crusades. We knights earned a reputation for valor and heroism and attracted many men of noble and merchant families to join us. Adventure was ours and our order grew wealthy; our cause sanctioned by the Pope. We were endorsed by the Roman Catholic Church, and we answered only to them and not to any king.

Phillipe IV, or as the people called him, Philip the Fair, ruled France as king. His reign was anything but fair. His nickname came from his appearance for he was tall and handsome; it had nothing to do with his actions as king. His power was great, but long and expensive wars with England had driven him deep into debt. Of course, kings have their own ways to raise money. He forcibly collected debts, forced the wealthy to lend him money and raised taxes on the people.

Truly, the plight of the common people did not concern him at all. He did not listen well. He was too busy talking to hear anyone but himself. He said all of the right things to the people, yet never followed through with the promises. In fact, many times what he did was exactly opposite to what had been said. He was a condescending egoist creating the best alliances for himself. He was corrupt and evil and because he was handsome and eloquent the people liked him. He fed on the ignorance of the masses.

The king relied heavily on a bureaucracy of legalists ill-qualified to make decisions for the kingdom. They were more concerned with policies that would pay off their constituents and line their pockets with gold. He left unpopular policy decisions to his finance ministers, distancing himself from any consequences. Much of his time was spent in the pursuits of pleasure: women, hunting and feasting. He was always working the politics of every situation to improve his personal standing of power and money, covertly of course, with spies in every area of the kingdom.

Against the advice of his more conservative advisors, the king decided to expel the Jewish peoples from France. He explained to the people that France could not tolerate the religious group any longer as it threatened the Catholic Church. He did not hear the people complain. Gaining confidence, he followed this act by expelling the Lombardi, loan-makers and bankers, who were called such because they were from that northern Italian region. Though the Jews and Lombardi had served an important purpose, the king claimed that they were immorally taking advantage of the French people; robbing the citizens with high interest rates and short loan terms while reaping great profits themselves. King Philip felt no remorse as he quietly confiscated the property of both groups forgiving himself of debt and adding much needed funds to pay down his debt with other groups.

Thus begins my personal story and charge: King Philip carefully targeted the Knights Templar, seeking to gain the power he did not control and searching for legitimate ways not only to cancel his huge debt with us, but also to seize the organization's wealth. He knew we had extensive interests in finance, shipping and importing as well as holding accumulated wealth from our members.

It is not well known, however, as the pilgrims readied themselves for the long trek to the Holy Land, we protected their wealth and luxuries in our castles. Upon their return, the pilgrims would sign over a portion of their wealth to us, in payment for their safe-keeping. Our order was very wealthy indeed; wealthier perhaps than the king. The Pope was kept very happy with a steady stream of gifts and homage from the Knights Templar.

I confess to you now one of my greatest secrets; the king was not entirely successful in taking our wealth from us. Of course, I do refer to the organization's wealth and not personal wealth – we did not own anything as part of our vow of poverty. Much of what the king wanted, we hid from him – to his grave disappointment.

{He took obvious pleasure in the fact that the king had much trouble in taking money from the Order.}

It was the Year of Our Lord 1298 and Jacques de Molay, my close friend, was named Knights Templar Grand Master. I did not envy his appointment. It was a position of power, prestige and political complexity. At this time the Crusades had not been going well. Our ranks had been reduced through unending fighting and our trade routes had been changed many times due to security issues. The Saracens had captured several critical posts. This tarnished our reputation somewhat with the middle and upper classes who were the very people helping to fund our efforts.

It was decided that we needed to rest, regroup and gather information. We stayed on the island of Cyprus, regaining our collective strength. We listened and waited for the opinion of the general public to shift and support our cause as stringently as in the past. We waited for reinforcements, for the second and third born sons to join our ranks and help with the continuation of the Crusades. Their inheritance and lands became ours and they would become part of our family.

Instead of public support, however, King Philip took advantage of public doubt and had his minions secretly spin lies about the Knights Templar. Indeed, the rumors spread far and wide as we know that bad news travels quickly. The general public had come to fear us and our secret rituals. The rumors seriously damaged our reputation. It was spread that we trampled the cross in our secret ceremonies and engaged in homosexual activities in our initiation ritual. The king convinced the Holy Church that they needed to investigate these charges firsthand as part of his plan.

In the meantime, Jacques was called to France to help with the funeral of the king's sister-in-law. He was suspicious, and yet, he went anyhow for how could he refuse? Exactly one day after the funeral, where Jacques served as a pall bearer, he was arrested. It was Friday, October 13, 1307. He was thrown into a dungeon on the charge of heresy. Under pressure from King Philip, the Pope ordered the arrest of all Templars throughout Christendom.

It was then that we came to know true suffering with the torture that first begins in the mind. They described graphically the things they would do to our loved ones if we did not confess to the horrible rumors they had heard. They promised us leniency in exchange for a confession, though we knew they lied. Sometimes we were interrogated alone and at times forced to watch others. We were deprived of sleep and held in cold stone cells lacking of daylight, fraught with the presence of rats and fleas with no foreseeable release.

When we were fed, it was stale, moldy bread and rancid water if there was any water at all. We worried most of all when they gave us decent food, as we came to know this was to help us gain our strength for hard questioning.

With the passing of time they developed a wider range of techniques to break us. Worst of all our torturers believed that they were on Our Heavenly Father's side in pursuit of truth. To make us bleed, to give us pain, made us clean; the more terrible the pain, the more righteous we became. They blessed their instruments of torture with holy water and absolved one another of their crimes of torture committed in the name of God.

It was usually quiet in the morning before they came for us. As the day wore on, the screams of pain and cries for mercy forced quiet with the rest of us. If we were quiet during torture then it was believed we had been aided by the devil – and the torture would worsen. We were always told what was about to happen to us and given a chance to confess to what the torturers wanted. Each round of torture was much worse than the one before.

I want you to understand what we experienced so that you can understand that it was no small thing. We were regularly deprived of our clothing. We were drawn up with cords from our wrists and whipped. Our wounds would just begin to heal and we would be whipped again. They burned us with hot irons. Our palms were nailed to boards. Our hands were scalded in pots of boiling oil. We endured this and much, much worse for three terrible years.

Some of us confessed…indeed many of us were broken. Even then, we endured further torture and hardship; but we knew brotherhood. We remained strong in our convictions and we knew we were innocent in this, the most terrible test of our faith in the One True God.

{*Aloysius retired for the evening with those final words. He was tired and I was tired. Torture is not something I can easily understand. It is the complete lack of humanity, of that which makes us different. Even animals do not harm each other for purpose, only for survival. He continued the next evening.*}

At the king's encouragement and blessing, and believing there was no hope to save them except through purifying fire, the Archbishop sentenced fifty-four of my brothers to be burnt at the stake on May 10, 1310. The burning took place outside of Paris and lasted two whole days. I prayed long hours and fasted for their souls and suffering. Saying goodbye was most terrible as we knew we would not see each other again on this earth. They would wait for us at Heaven's Gate. This terrible event broke the spirit and power of the Knights Templar as we had known it. I did not know what judgment would await me – or any of the leaders – as it had yet to be decided by the Pope. We waited in prison for four more long years.

Life imprisonment was the judgment passed on March 18, 1314. This was not what Jacques had expected. Realizing that we could not survive much more imprisonment, Jacques recanted his earlier confession obtained during one terrible torture session. He thought this would give us one last audience with the Archbishop. We both proclaimed our order's innocence for the final time. We received no final words with anyone. The king was beyond furious.

Philip the Fair ordered us both to be burned at the stake. He was finally getting what he wanted: complete disablement of the Order in France while laying claim to our wealth and power. It was outrageous and deceitful, not concerning religion or God…concerning only money and power.

Sometimes decisions and policies are created under the guise of helping the common people when truly those in power grow rich from the exploitation of their duties. There is a lesson in this; look to motive in your dealings in all things. Ask questions and do not be led blindly. Who stands to gain or lose in any situation? What are the true motives for each party involved?

When it comes time to face death, the only thing that matters is your truth. How did you live? Were you honest? Loyal? Worthy of trust? Did you protect the innocent and quash the evil-doer? These are matters of importance; be aware that one person can make all the difference for good or evil to those that surround them and beyond.

To incur the wrath of a king has a most terrible consequence. I was greatly somber, for to be sentenced to death is the gravest of affairs. To have the execution carried out immediately was both a blessing and a curse. There was no time for farewells. I don't even remember being taken to the tiny island on the River Seine where we were to be burned.

A great crowd had gathered to watch as the news had spread quickly through the city. Most of the poor believed that we were innocent, especially after seeing the terrible spectacle that had happened four years earlier to my fifty-four brethren. The usual jeers and taunts at executions were noticeably absent as we arrived. I'm sure this angered the king further.

The pyre was built and awaited only us. We knelt down, back to back, so that we might pray to God for a quick and merciful death. Yet we knew it would be terrible and slow. Jacques asked the executioner not to gag him as he slipped a gold coin in his hand; he said that he wanted to pray aloud for forgiveness. I did not ask the same; my hands and feet were bound and I was gagged with a rag of cloth. I did not trust that I would be able to remain in the fire. As the hay was lit, and the smoke and heat began, I heard Jacques cry out to the king, "I summon you, King Phillip and you Pope Clement, to meet me before God in his great kingdom within one year to be judged for your crimes! Vekam, Adonai!"

I choose not to share the agony we endured. I was glad for death, the sweet dark angel, when she finally descended to take our souls to heaven. Only I did not go. I watched as they ascended knowing I had further work to do before resting.

The Lord did summon both King Philip and Pope Clement with death within the following year. I would like to have seen that meeting.

Alas, I was not there...

The King's Frustration

On our Grand Master de Molay's orders, on the night before his initial arrest, a procession consisting of five wagons of straw left the Temple in Paris. One of the drivers was my friend, the disguised Preceptor of France. These wagons had been secretly loaded with important documents, gold and all manner of collected treasures from our ventures in the Middle East. Horses had to be exchanged along the route in order to replace the exhausted animals during the trip. To where, you might ask? They traveled day and night to a sleepy port town in the north of France.

Our ships, which fashioned the largest armada in the West, were docked in our home port in La Rochelle. They were ordered by secret messenger to leave port quickly and quietly in the middle of the night to make for the Iberian Coast. Three ships departed the main armada and sailed to a port in the north of France, for a secret rendezvous.

Imagine the king's anger when the militia reported back that the port at La Rochelle was empty. The entire Templar fleet was gone. Can you see why torture was inflicted upon us and why it lasted for so many years? The king sought the whereabouts of our fortune of treasure. Understand now of the reason why de Molay was the most horribly tortured among us. The king knew that de Molay had given the orders for the fleet's departure, yet, only after many years of torture did he concede that de Molay did not know where the ships had eventually docked. Thus de Molay did not know where the Templar treasures were hidden and his usefulness was spent. The king ordered his death at the first opportunity.

The Heresy of the Shroud

Let me be succinct and direct: the face seen on the Shroud of Turin is that of Jacques de Molay and not that of Jesus Christ of Nazareth. The cloth that has come to be known as the shroud had been used to cover and carry de Molay after a particularly horrendous torture session.

De Molay had been stripped of his clothing and whipped. Then, in order to punish him for his supposed sin of trampling the cross and denying Christ's death, the torturers pushed a crown of thorns on his head. They laughed at the irony as the blood trickled down his face. Finally, they nailed him to a cross, and though they did not wish to kill him, they did crudely crucify him. Our torturers saw the crucifixion as most appropriate for the Grand Master and invited many members of high rank within the church to observe it.

It takes a very long time to die on the cross. He was there for many hours, yet not long enough to die. We suffered as we saw his suffering. Under this terrible duress, de Molay confessed to the crimes against the church. The torturers took him down so he could sign a document of confession. A church cleric had to hold his hand to make the signing readable. Blood stained the white paper and I hoped the Pope who had once been de Molay's friend would see it and know what torture that he had resigned de Molay to endure.

Such torture is hard on the physical body. It changes the chemicals that constitute us. Sweat, dirt and blood covered de Molay's body. When they took him down and laid him out, there was no strength left in him, only anguish and pain. Several Templar witnesses, including myself, were called to care for him. They did not want him to die yet. We wrapped him in this cloth, now called the Shroud, so that we could carry him to his cell. He was alive, but barely. What you see on the Shroud of Turin is the impression of de Molay's face and body created as we took him to his dungeon chamber.

In 1353, John the Good endorsed my grand nephew Geoffroy de Charnay, who was named after me, to build a church in the Town of Lirey. The small church was consecrated in 1356. Four months later, my grand nephew was killed in battle. His widow, a woman of some standing who was of a fine nature, looked into her deceased husband's possessions to see what she might sell in order to continue running the household without remarrying too soon.

She found the old shroud and carefully unfolded it. Mystified, she saw the image of a man who might have resembled Christ. Although she knew it was the image of Jacques de Molay, she quickly concluded that she and their church could profit greatly if it were considered a relic. She displayed it as a relic in the Lirey church without anyone's permission.

The Church knew that the shroud's image was that of de Molay and not that of Jesus; the widow was ordered to destroy the shroud. She chose to hide it rather than destroy it. After later remarrying a nobleman with excellent standing in the Church, she was able to consider displaying the shroud once more. She did so many years later with the blessing of the Pope, who was none other than her nephew through marriage.

In fact, the Pope agreed to look the other way for one simple reason: it was essential that the identity of the man who left his impression on the cloth not be discovered as that of Jacques de Molay. At the time, Jacques de Molay was routinely considered a holy martyr of high standing and the Church risked being swept away by a new cult focused on de Molay, whose story was comparable to that of Jesus Christ.

As the black plague swept across the Christian world, the public looked to the Church for guidance and salvation. The Church provided the Shroud of Turin in answer to the cries for comfort and hope. Saying the cloth had been recently discovered in the treasures in the Pope's keeping, they directed believers to look upon it's wonder and see the very face of Jesus Christ. People who saw the Shroud claimed miracles and the Shroud became a known relic. Of course, only those at the highest levels of the Church knew the truth. The truth, known in such small circles, is easily lost or hidden.

This I witnessed with mine own eyes. Seeing this is what I chose instead of meeting my family in heaven…yet, I know now that my story and secrets shall be told. I take my leave of you now. Please consider my words carefully and always keep your eyes open.

{At this, I felt his presence leave and have not felt it since. I am certain that he has gone and has already chosen to reincarnate and participate in our world again today. He has much to share.}

Li Ying

1915 in the Xian Region of China

I felt humbled in this dream state on April 2, 2010. I accompanied a young woman of approximately 15 years of age. I saw through her eyes the sadness and loss of life in the villages through which she passed. There were children and elderly people going about their daily household chores, however, I noted a missing generation of men and women of healthy age. Sickness of a strange sort had attacked the middle-aged population and left the young and old mostly unscathed. It was an epidemic of disease thought to be punishment from evil spirits.

We traveled with her grandfather who was a known medical practitioner. He worked with traditional methods of healing such as acupuncture and medicinal herbology. He held closely to the old ways.

I could feel the young woman's internal conflict; she was a woman and young, but she felt she had ideas that her grandfather should consider. She wanted to contribute to his work instead of being, in effect, his servant. She had yet to find her voice. In that time and place, women had no voice. Her story is conveyed below using the voice she has finally found.

Student Becomes Teacher

I am but a young woman but I learn quickly. I assist the doctor. As I walk behind him along this dirt road, he is thinking out loud. He is deeply troubled, trying to understand the nature and mystery of the sickness. We walk and I listen to him. We walk between villages following the path of death, examining those who are sick and dying. He has tried many methods of treatment. All methods have failed so far, though a few have offered some level of comfort in the final hours.

He is perplexed. He stops for a brief moment and I hear him say under his breath "...because the sickness presents so many unusual ways, we have misdiagnosed it as rice-water disease (cholera), three-week fever (typhoid) and the bone-ache fever (dengue fever); these are mistaken." He scratched his beard and began to walk forward once again.

"We know that the disease does not normally strike the old, the sick or the young--it strikes hardest at the healthy members of society, which makes no sense," he stated with confusion.

The road before us was deserted. Everyone is scared to go about, for they may be attacked by the unseen and disturbed gods of nature. They live in everything, every tree and field and meadow. No one knows what was done to upset them or how they can be appeased. No one wants to get sick.

The doctor spoke in a louder voice, but did not direct his words to me, "When you can begin to see the blue color moving from the ears and spreading over the face, then there is no saving them and we can only give comfort. It is then only a matter of a few hours until death comes."

I silently nod. He is the doctor and I have much to learn. I have not, to date, told him of my personal observations. It is not my place. My duty is to assist and not interfere. I am not qualified to offer any opinion unless he might ask...and he will not. Though he is my grandfather, he is a man and a doctor first; therefore he is very powerful. I am nothing but a burden on my parents. I am blessed to be able to serve my family in this manner.

I have noticed that as the disease takes its course, the symptoms follow a pattern. This is knowledge that the doctor has already acquired. The illness affects a person in the following way. First there is a high fever followed by tremors, coughing and pain in the muscles. Sometimes the sufferer will experience a sore throat, but there is always fatigue. The victim loses strength so much so that they cannot eat or drink without assistance. In the final stage, there is troubled and shallow breathing followed closely by death. There is no known cure.

What I have come to know and consider as important is that the people who are becoming ill are also those who are responsible for the day-to-day activities that control the many aspects of village life. These are the merchants, bakers, butchers and tailors who work and meet one another; people who spread the sickness to each other... spreading death. Elderly people and infants do not go out from the house very often.

Someday, I would like to inform the doctor of these facts. Nevertheless, I know he will not ask my opinion. For fear of shaming my family and being sent home, I will keep to my job of cooking, cleaning and making the appropriate travel preparations. Should I feel the urge to open my mouth, I will bite my hand to remind me of my place; I am a servant. I am hobbled already, as my feet were bound as a baby, and walking is a difficult chore. The binding made my feet stay smaller than they should be, but it will help the matchmaker find a husband of good familial status. Nonetheless, I am lucky that my mother and father decided that I should live. Not all girl babies are as lucky as I have been. I have seen many left to die in fields alone. There is no compassion for them.

{There is a pause here as she gathered her energy to continue the telling of her story.}

If I could have spoken freely, I think that conceivably many lives would have been saved. Unfortunately, when I became sick, I did not have the strength to tell him. In life, I never had the strength or character to talk to him. The truth cuts through the darkness of ignorance; however, it takes courage to speak it. There are consequences when the truth is spoken and consequences when it is not spoken. I lost my opportunity when I succumbed to the disease.

I would have married next year. I had been blessed with life and servitude to my family, even if I thought my mind was useful, I would never have had need of it. I wanted to have children of my own, and I would have made sure that my daughters, if I had been blessed with any, lived. Love alone is reason to live. I would have taught my daughters the secret that I know; that women are as smart as men and should have the ability to work alongside them in their vocations. More than this, at times, women are better at some tasks than men. Alas, my musings died with me.

My message to you is this: if someone has power, or the illusion of power, you must still follow your own sense of right and wrong and give direction according to your true thoughts – even if that person is not used to hearing the truth. If everyone always tells that person what they want to hear, then hearing the truth will have an effect on them. It could be anger, so prepare for it. They could outright reject everything you suggest, and it might be an unpleasant experience for you. How they deal with what you say is not your business; you have stayed true to yourself and said what needed to be said in order to maintain your own balance. You have also given that person something to think about, and perhaps, from which to learn. The opportunity to learn is all that we can ask in life; to help someone learn is a great honor.

I was buried in a grave with many others far from my home. My parents, I think, did not mourn my loss. They lost nothing when I died. My brothers had already secured government jobs and their wives would carry out the familial piety requirements. In essence, my parents would enjoy the rest of their lives and upon their death, their spirits and resting place would be well serviced with the many required gifts, cleaning and visits. No one even knew where I was buried.

In my next life, for which I have long awaited the tide of public opinion to start to change, I will be someone who speaks her mind with honesty at all times; not with anger, but with directness and conviction. Watch for me, I shall not be silent.

Gracie and Friedrich

1950 at the Ehrenberg Ruins in Bavaria

I was staying in southern Indiana for a few days on a short vacation. Not many people may realize it, but several areas in southern Indiana are largely populated with German descendant Americans who are very proud of their heritage. It should have been no surprise, then, that I spent the better part of an hour talking with a lovely, yet deceased, woman named Gracie early on the morning of July 11, 2009. She spoke at length about her friend Friedrich and his great interest in castles in Bavaria.

Gracie was quite an eccentric personality. She had been wealthy in her previous life and though she had crossed over, she chose to surround us with the things that made her comfortable and happy. In my dream I actually arrived at her huge European inspired stone mansion in a sleek new Rolls Royce.

We drove up a long curved drive around a beautiful green courtyard in the center of which was a large fountain. There was a mermaid in the center of the fountain being continually bathed from several water-spewing fish. We stopped in front of the mansion and its many stone steps leading up to great double wooden doors. As the driver opened the car door for me, I noticed that I was wearing a gorgeous mink coat. I realized then that it was a gift from my host to keep me warm in the cool late autumn air. It was luxurious.

The manor was richly decorated and housed a great many historical artifacts. I was shown to an antiquated library, which smelled like antique books and surely held stacks of written treasures and manuscripts. As I sat down opposite my host in a large leather wingback chair, she began to tell me about her group of friends and their many interests, mostly historical and archaeological in nature. She smiled warmly as she conveyed that she had tried a great many times to speak to others and had never made any connection. She was so pleased that we were able to communicate.

Gracie had reached a point where she wasn't choosing to be born as often; she was akin to a shepherd for a few souls with whom she deeply resonated. Friedrich was one of those souls. Gracie would occasionally choose to incarnate in order to help others more so than herself.

Friedrich joined us after the initial pleasantries had been exchanged. He was deeply troubled and had much to say to society at large. He did not sit down, but paced the floor with anxious energy. He was, however, to me a handsome man with dark hair and eyes who wore the fashion of the 1920's with much style and grace. Much to Gracie's dismay, he had been refusing to incarnate until his message had been conveyed. His story begins in the next section. I would like to convey that Friedrich is an advanced soul going through a dilemma of self versus society.

Gracie has explained to me that Earth is a place for us to learn and choice provides the challenging situations; at no time will any person on Earth decide to make the right choice every time. That circumstance does not exist, for if it did, we would not need to be here having already reached nirvana enlightenment.

Friedrich would like to believe that society-at-large could be taught a concept and then remember it in the collective consciousness thereby foregoing the need to learn it again. He had not yet accepted that individuals with free choice constitute society. Individuals have the choice to learn and grow beyond their limitations, thereby improving society. Yet, this generation of individuals die, returning in new bodies at random, and all the while, new souls are born and being integrated into society and must choose their paths. Knowledge is gained and lost in between the generations. This suggestion is a source of great lamentation for Friedrich.

Technology is something that improves with each generation and humans keep record of it and advance. It is a linear concept. Humanity, which I will define as kindness, respect and love for our fellow human, is individual in nature. This concept of humanity flexes with the character of new souls being born and the amount of time that the previous generation devotes to the guiding of the new generation. This is a very familial process not bound by genetics, but by the mix of old and new souls in each generation.

Society learns, loses knowledge and then re-learns; history does repeat itself over and again. Humanity is a continual process that takes time; we cannot record it and advance. We must know it in our hearts and teach it to our children through practice and example and at times, discipline.

Friedrich's thoughts and ideas add much to our culture on Earth, so on a personal note, I hope he returns soon. The following story is told in Friedrich's own words.

Activity and Rest

My father was a shipping merchant. I travelled with him and was his apprentice. The world was my classroom and experience my teacher. I was not schooled formally, but I learned all that I needed to know on those ocean crossings and merchant dealings. I could read and write as well as navigate by the stars and draft courses for the ship. I had a good working knowledge of people and cultures.

My father was a smart and shrewd man, but a kind man, too. He showed me how to live soundly and think for myself. He respected himself and others in business dealings and his personal life. I knew to treat men fairly, children with kindness and women with great respect all by the time I was ten. Some children do not get such guidance; I am grateful for it still.

We travelled much and I came to know a great many foreign lands. As much as Asia and its ports were exotic and mysterious, European ports were familiar and much like home. I took many opportunities to travel inland during our time in port, usually as we were waiting for cargo to arrive or when seeking out new merchants with whom to deal business.

My favorite place to visit were the Ehrenberg castle ruins. They were isolated and serene, and more than that, I felt that the very land itself was alive and sentient...in a state of dreaming and resting. I was comforted. At one time there had been much activity in that place and now it was time to rest and perhaps reflect.

The first time I visited, I only had time to see the lower ruins which dated back to the thirteenth century. I was seemingly alone as I ate my lunch of bread, cheese and wine; however, I took company with the memories that haunted the shadows of that place. I imagined what it would have been like to live in this place along with the knights that defended its walls. I must have been seventeen at the time. The spirit of that place was tangible, even though I had no true knowledge of what I was feeling.

I visited again three years later and climbed to the second ruin which was not as old. This one I hadn't seen before, yet I had one of the most splendid experiences of my life. When I reached the crest of the hill, I found myself deep inside old-growth forest. It was only after I had explored for quite a while that I realized that the forest was, in fact, encompassing the fortress. It had been long since overgrown by several hundred years of abandonment. I cannot adequately describe the tranquility I found that afternoon. I sat in the cool shade surrounded by the nature that had conquered the indomitable fortress. I never had time to return to this place in my living years, but now that I have passed, I return from time to time to this place as it comforts me.

Imagine my loathing, when I returned recently, to see that electric lights had been added to the ruins so that they would be visible at night. I had crossed over after a long and fulfilling life, but I had always wanted to see this place one final time. I wanted to experience the energy once more before I left the earthly plane to begin my life on the Other Side. This place had brought me much serenity, such that I carried the memory of it in my heart and it was a source of peace.

To see the upper ruins, one had to ascend several steep paths. Part of the charm was that not many people really wanted to walk so difficult a path to see the old castle ruins. Now, I suppose, the "problem" has been fixed. Even the upper ruins can be plainly seen in due large part to the clear cutting of the old growth forest that has taken place. It is a travesty. The experience has been completely destroyed because of slothfulness. The land is disturbed and the peace is gone.

It is the saddest fact that the stumps of the forest are all that remain, like reminders of torture inflicted upon the land. This ground and the memories that reside here now suffer great exposure. All of this was done so that the ruins would be visible from the thoroughfare below in an effort to attract tourists. No longer is this a cool place of reflection; the hot sun beats down on a hilltop of weeds.

Worse, the ruins are being rebuilt using contemporary materials and practices. Whatever the eventual goal, the short term goal is inspired by money. Money is fleeting; you cannot take it with you to the grave. It must be earned in the proper way or it does damage to your karmic responsibilities.

Everything has its time, its use and purpose and then it is to rest...to be peaceful. Even places need to rest in order to provide a balance. We should recognize this concept and not interfere.

I will leave you now that I have spoken the thoughts that have kept me here. I know not how many times society must learn this concept. There is a time for activity and a time for rest; that is the balance we must achieve in our private lives as well as for the world at large.

8

Accounts Of The Other Side

Light and Consciousness

Many people wonder what awaits them after death...it is the great mystery of what lies beyond. Do heaven and hell exist? Is there a purgatory where we must wait? Do we cease to exist?

The stories in this chapter will enlighten and hopefully comfort you. The afterlife becomes a place of learning instead of judgment. The Creator Source is no longer a punishing god demanding obedience; rather, you become your own evaluator. It is your own progress that you help or hinder. Time on Earth becomes less stressed, knowing that you do not have to become perfect in one lifetime.

The fact is that sometimes we mess up...sometimes we screw up our entire lives; the question becomes, how do you recover? Be comforted because you are not here alone; your ancestors support you and your angels, guides and unseen helpers surround and encourage you to keep moving forward. We are all part of the Creator Source, the divine; there is always hope even when we think there may be none.

The situation on our Earth is constantly changing, but we have the ability to change ourselves and influence those around us for better or worse. It is a daily decision that we choose consciously or unconsciously. The following stories make it known to us that we should start consciously choosing our paths and recognize the power we have and seek help from our guides and angels whenever we need it.

Lisa

1990 in the Great Lakes Region of the United States

Early on the morning of May 30, 2009, I watched from the side of the road next to a frozen river bank as a car struggled to pull free from the broken ice. It had slid off of an ice covered country road. The rear end of the car was submerging rather quickly. Others stood near; watching as the car was pulled into the current. Now it became confusing, because as the car, in reality, moved further into the river, I saw a very large Light Being – what I would consider an Angel, step forward and grasp the car at the front, pick it up easily and set it down on the riverbank.

I also watched as the real car sunk beneath the freezing water, upending over itself a few times as it was tugged along in the swiftly flowing current. Then I saw the Light Being open the door and allow the driver, Lisa, to exit. I was sure there had been two people inside the car, a man named Tom and his girlfriend Lisa. I hadn't been wrong, and yet only Lisa died, so this requires some further explanation. This is an example of one of the few times that I did not experience the death – no cold water, no difficulty breathing, just the picture I described above and the explanation in Lisa's words below.

After Death Conversation

Tom and I weren't supposed to be together that night…or at all, really. My parents did not approve of our inter-racial relationship. This didn't matter to us because we had love; the kind that breaks your heart when you can't be together. We knew we were right for one another even as the world, well, my world it seemed, knew it was completely wrong.

I had a fight with my dad that evening. It was about Tom. Yes, he had been staying over at my place. No, we weren't married. No, we didn't have any plans to get married. NO, I WAS NOT PREGNANT. God, how embarrassing and frustrating and so none of their business! I had not lived at home for several years. I had met Tom at college and we had been seeing each other for awhile...a lot longer than my parents knew. I had dreaded the way I knew they would treat him and tried to save him the anger and humiliation. He never truly believed they would reject him. He was wrong.

I had gone home for dinner to see if we could at least be civil about the decisions I was making for myself. I tried to ask them not to judge Tom on his skin color; but worse, it seemed they were judging me for my acceptance of him (when I had such a *promising* future ahead of me). I begged them to look beyond something so superficial. It is what is on the inside that makes us who we are – that is what they taught me to believe. What hypocrites! Oh, it's okay to talk to people "like that", but not okay to be involved with them? Unbelievable and shallow...that's what I said to my dad that caused him to grab me by the shoulders, tow me to the front door and push me out...without my coat...without my purse and it was fifteen degrees and snowing. I only had the car keys in my pocket.

I stayed on the porch for awhile, crying while I listened to the yelling inside. My mom was saying to let me in and my dad's booming voice refusing and disowning me. I was angry that my mom wouldn't stand up to my dad and just unlock the door. When I lost hope that he would let me back in, and when I was too cold to fight it anymore, I got in my car and left.

Of course, I was going straight to Tom; yes crying and definitely driving too fast. He knew how much this dinner had meant to me. It was a final reach and then we were going to simply live our lives without their involvement. Tom and I had bought a condo and we were going to move in together. I hadn't even had a chance to tell them. Of course, this meant I would be moving away to the city. I had just graduated from college and landed a job that had agreed to transfer me near to where Tom was already working. It was only about 3 hours away from my home town, so I would still be able to see my parents.

Sadly, it was not meant to be. I took a corner too fast and ended up in the river. I was scared out of my mind! I couldn't get my door open and I couldn't get any traction to get out of the river, either. When the water started seeping in and the car shifted backwards into the river, I lost self-control. I panicked and screamed for help. Almost immediately I saw Tom sitting next to me; he had come to me – appeared from nowhere! He reached out and held my face with his hand. He shook his head back and forth gently, and then nodded toward the front of the car.

I think my mouth must have gaped open when I saw the enormous radiant white angel standing at the front of the car; yes with wings and everything! He picked the car up and out of the water with one hand and lightly set it down on the riverbank. My angel opened the door to the car and helped me out. Then I remembered to close my mouth and say thank you. Tom was no longer with me at this time. It was then that I noticed all of the others who were standing next to the road. I was confused somewhat, yet I was so happy to see my grandparents, and they were smiling, and yet, they were supposed to be dead; had died years ago! So, I was dead, right? It happened so quickly, so unexpectedly…and so painlessly! I guess I wasn't going back, you know, no body means no resuscitation. Now what? The question had but formed in my mind when the angel departed heavenward in a great flash of light, making a circular opening of light that gently pulled at my hair…like a gentle breeze.

A woman that stood a little apart from the group stepped forward. Strangely, it was the middle of winter and I hadn't noticed her bright green garb or bare feet; most notable is that she did not look the least bit cold. I examined her mocha skin, dark hair and feral cat-like eyes; she was exotic, beautiful and familiar. She spoke to me without words, relaying that she was my guide. I knew her name was Alejandra. I knew she would help me.

I was sad that my life and all its future and potential had ended. I was really sad about not seeing Tom again. Even though I wanted to go see him, Alejandra had other plans. I just thought, this sucks, now what?

{Lisa has been asked to focus on certain elements of her story so that she will convey what she is being allowed to share with us.}

I have to be careful about what I say in this part of my story because not all of it can be told. Some things you just have to find out after you get here; but trust me, this is a good place. The longer I'm here, the more I remember – about my past and about the people with whom I've been working. Let me start at the beginning.

I made the decision to go through the circular opening and, to my surprise, I simply rose up off of the ground and was gently tugged inside. It felt like a full body warm air massage…sort of like being gently scrubbed… and it was absolutely fantastic! After a time, I arrived to the other side and felt incredibly light and wonderful. I was in a white area and was openly greeted by my grandparents and many people that I didn't even know – who obviously knew me!

I found out later that these were members of my "group" – souls that regularly work together in order to help one another advance. I did eventually remember all of them; it just took some adjustment time and rest for everything to come back to me.

After my homecoming, Alejandra ushered me into a small but pleasant room near where I had arrived. It was cozy and intimate lit with firelight and smelling of incense. Painted clay pots referencing Nazca lines decorated the small room. I was immediately at ease – like I could almost remember some other happy time in another life. The room had a soft dirt floor, comfortable dark green cushions on which to sit and a fire pit in the center of the room. Liquid simmered in a small kettle over the fire. I sat down on an inviting cushion and the scent of the herbal liquid became recognizable. I sat down as Alejandra poured the drink, yerba mate, into small clay cups. I sipped it and was soothed.

The following is a portion of our conversation. I didn't think I could tell it in any other way except directly. It was powerful for me as I learned so much. I won't be following this conversation with any further details.

I want my parents to know how much I love them. I know they must feel much guilt about the situation, but they shouldn't. I want them to realize that I was in their lives to challenge them. We made a deal before I chose to be born to them. I was to challenge my father to open his mind and move him away from old patterns of thought. He had been involved in the slave trade in several past lives and needed to overcome his prejudices.

I was also to challenge my mom to stand up for herself and how she believes. She has to know that she has power; she just has to realize it! I'm not sad that I died. In fact, we kind of knew that it was a possibility from the beginning. We knew that it would take something incredibly strong and shocking to help my chosen parents to change at their core. I had been hoping that it wouldn't take my death to change them.

Dad, don't be angry at Tom anymore. I still love him and nothing was his fault. Honor me and yourself by showing Tom respect and kindness. Please do this for me. I am reaching out to you from beyond death because

I want you to grow beyond who you are. You are ready for this change. I am waiting for both of you, mom and dad, and look forward to NEW challenges…I don't want to do this one again.

Alejandra: You have done well.

Me: I don't know what you're talking about. I'm really just trying to understand what's going on. I feel overwhelmed.

Alejandra: Let's go over a few things to help you remember. You were born to loving parents, parents in soul groups other than your own that needed help. You really challenged them and a few of their archaic beliefs. That's what you were supposed to do, and you did it effortlessly, just by being yourself!

Me: But I died! Now I won't have the chance to be with Tom. Now what will he do? What will I do?

Alejandra: I know you've been though some trauma, but we have all gone through traumatic events. We recover and we learn from our good decisions and our mistakes and then we do it all again, hopefully better the next time. So, you will get another chance. I know you don't realize this, but your death has allowed Tom to address some issues he needs to during this life and also allows you to take some much needed rest. You see, you exited your body knowing that it was time to move on…you didn't stay to go through the final uncomfortable feelings of death. We do have that choice if only we remember. Earth is such a wonderful planet to choose to work on, yet it is one of the most difficult.

Close your eyes for a moment and listen to my voice. You will remember more quickly if you are relaxed. Let me explain a bit more. You often work with Tom and, unfortunately, it rarely has a successful outcome in life. Here, in the Life Between Lives, you are in the same soul group and have always resonated with each other…of course you love each other… but part of it is that you are both very alike. It's not enough to simply challenge yourselves; both of you take it that step further by accepting difficult circumstances and restrictions in life. You have both grown through these circumstances much more quickly than by choosing easy lives. Therein lies the issue; tumultuous lives can be unpredictable and short. The fact is that you both laugh and tease one another about things that seem so tough when you're on Earth.

Me: Life is hard on Earth; why is that so? Because even now, as we sit here in this *pretend* room and I can smell the *pretend* tea in my cup and feel the soft *pretend* floor under my feet, I feel I am really breathing for the first time! Though I'm fairly certain I don't have to breathe here, right?

Alejandra: I know it seems a pretend room; yet, it is really a reorganization of energy that you can see, hear, feel, taste and smell. The tea is quite delicious, but it is not tea in the traditional sense; you won't really drink it, but you can savor the essence. As well, you can see that we don't have physical bodies, yet I can sense you and feel your essence… in many ways the mingling of our energies have a much more intimate feeling than our physical bodies on Earth can. However, you can feel another person's energy and essence on Earth but it is much less obvious within a human shell.

I chose this setting, which you may not remember yet, because it was our home many lifetimes ago when we were sisters. It was such a happy time. You see, when we return from a hard life or death, we need to be comforted. This place should feel familiar and evoke good feelings for you.

Me: You're right. The oppressive emotions I had been feeling are fading. I feel released and happy. I'm content not to be fighting against anything at the moment.

Alejandra: That's because you don't have the demands that come with a body…eat, sleep, exercise, providing for your loved ones, taking care of your health; those are all stresses that you don't have here. This is the beginning of your resting phase; then it is a time to reflect, learn and have fellowship and relaxation before returning to an active state once again… being reborn!

Me: How much time do I have before I go back?

Alejandra: Time is irrelevant here. You simply go back when you are ready. Sometimes you've gone back right away and sometimes you've waited a hundred Earth years. You will know when you are ready...for now, it is time to rest.

Elizabeth

1920 in the Southeast Region of the United States

All was in darkness except for a sliver of daylight coming through drawn curtains on the far side of a single white hospital bed. There was a record player on the bedside table. The music had long since finished. The sound of the needle static had brought us into the room.

A person was lying in the bed, not moving, tucked-in tight with white blankets. I was with Lizzie, watching the person in the bed, slightly afraid yet wanting to help. It was her mother, Caroline, and she was very sick. Almost as quickly as we had entered the room, a young nurse came and reprimanded us for coming into the room with dirty shoes.

"Out, out, go out and play and don't come in here unless your father says you can," she said quietly through the white mask that covered her face.

The following is an account of Lizzie's experience. Present time for me was October 13, 2010.

Group Leader

We had been to the pool a lot that summer, my mother and me. We were very close. I turned 9-years-old and was very proud of myself for being able to swim across the entire pool. My mom would watch and count the time for me. My record was 21 seconds; very fast in my estimation. That seems like a long time ago. It is part of a jumble of memories of my past life on Earth.

My mother had been sick with the polio virus. About a week after she had fallen ill, a fever began in my poor body. It was not a physically strong body anyhow; it was smaller and weaker than those I had chosen in previous lives. I had never really experienced true sickness until this lifetime.

While my mother recovered from the fever, headache and pain, the exhaustion of the illness stayed with her. The doctors said that it could continue for the rest of her life. As she became healthier, I became sicker.

My memories of this sickness are fading even as I tell you this story. I do know that it was a terrible circumstance. My parents' worried faces standing at the door to my room, the white-coated doctor with the perfect pirate's beard who poked and prodded me and finally the nurse that had previously scolded me who now looked at me with her big brown doe eyes full of pity. I was in a pitiful state.

A week or more after the fever began, it was determined that I had the breathing polio. It was a terrible illness. At the end, I was unable to move my arms or legs, nor could I swallow without great difficulty. I was to go to the hospital the following day for treatment; my body gave up trying to breathe that night. It was as if I had been in a nightmare, trapped inside a prison of a body that would not obey my will to breathe. The next moment, I was free, exhaled in a final breath. I know this seems a quick story, but I have many things to convey. My death is not as important as my experiences after death.

My mother was asleep in the chair next to my bed. I touched her hand and discovered the source of her exhaustion…the illness had taken a toll; however, a new life was beginning to grow inside her! It would be a good reason for her to continue to recover and not get lost in her sadness over me. It would be a strong baby, healthy and smart. I was happy to know that I would have a brother or sister.

I remember the crossing over. I have completed this act many times, so I wasn't worried about where to go. I didn't need any assistance. I just looked for the portal and it was there, spinning above my head. I surrendered myself to it and traversed the short distance to the other side. Really there wasn't any true distance to travel, it was the cleansing in the tunnel that helped to clarify my energy, clean it so that I wouldn't feel as disoriented as I might otherwise feel.

No one met me in the gathering area when I arrived. I didn't expect to see anyone. I had long since stopped needing to receive consultation after my arrival. I went straight through the area and exited the busy room of reunions. I am not sure how to explain this area, except to say that it is full of stratified light. I am able to see the layers and know that each strand will take me almost instantly to another place. I but touch the strand I need and I am transported with a swiftness that is not describable to the human experience to the place of the Council.

It is here that I speak with the Council about my life just lived. We talk about the choices I made and the hardships I experienced, however, there is no judgment such as you might expect. In this life between lives, I believe that we judge ourselves more harshly than could any guide or council member. The Council, of whom there are five assigned to me, points out my successes and makes recommendations for my next life, including suitable challenges and physical orientation.

My guide is at this meeting of the Council. I am very happy to see her. She comes to me quickly after the meeting finishes and tells me that there is no time to lose! This is a strange concept, of time in the afterlife, because for us time does not pass. Time continues on Earth, but it does not age us or progress on the Other Side.

It had been decided by the Elder Group and Council Members that I should reincarnate on Earth as soon as possible. My Group Members were incarnating at this very moment and I was to incarnate with them so that we could work together and help each other. Let me explain a bit further before we continue.

First, the choice to incarnate is always ours. We can take the advice of the senior groups or we can choose to ignore it. The consequences are ours alone to bear in either case. I give value to the advice I receive from them as they are in a place that I have not yet reached, but aspire to achieve.

Second, when our souls are created, taken from the very Source of All That Is (you may call the source God or Goddess but there is no gender orientation), we are placed in a group of similar souls. It is in this group that we learn best; we learn from each other's mistakes and successes. Sometimes a group member will surpass the group and move on into another group. At times, a group member may take longer to learn what the group has already learned and will join another more suitable group in which they can better learn.

In my case, I am the Group Leader. There are seven in my group, each unique and gifted, as are all souls. We work very well together. I have spent many lifetimes with them in various roles. However, there are numerous groups and oftentimes we work together for learning purposes. For example, my mother in the previous lifetime was a member of another group. Her challenge in that lifetime was to overcome depression. She had committed suicide in several previous lives.

We can never fully know how we will learn lessons or how we will help each other learn lessons. Our souls recognize each other for who we truly are though our bodies may or may not. We may feel an attraction or need to take some action on behalf of another person and not understand fully why we are doing it. This is soul recognition. Pay attention for there is deep meaning in this and what you or someone else will learn could change your lives forever.

I didn't ask many questions as we made our way towards the staging area for departures. It had been three months since my Earthly physical death. I like surprises, so I just trusted that my next life would be interesting and completed with the members of my group in full participation.

Imagine my surprise as I waved goodbye, stepped into the departure area, and arrived back at the same place of my death! I was to bond with the baby I had made previous contact with – the baby in my mother's womb. I was to continue with her, help her on her journey and spend a lifetime surrounded by my close friends.

I crossed over last year in 2010 while in my nineties. Much can be learned in a long life. Growing old has its own set of challenges, especially for the vain and those of us who may be frail in body but strong in mind. Truly, I could not have asked for more, and yet, I will take some time to recover before I return again. Farewell and I hope that you have learned something from my experience that comforts you. It is sad to think that there are people who believe in nothing after death. I wish to offer you some hope.

Naoki

1985 in the Southeast Region of the United States

I saw the front of the car crumple from the passenger's seat. The entire front of the sleek red sports car folded like aluminum foil underneath the rear of the SUV in front of us. The SUV had stopped without warning, skidded but hit nothing in front of it. The driver of the car, a male college foreign exchange student, never had a chance. His body was wedged behind and underneath the steering wheel, which had been bent and crushed under the rear end of the SUV due to the fact that the little car had been hit from behind by a full-size truck.

The accident had happened incredibly fast and occurred very early in the morning. The female driver of the SUV, also a college student, had been out drinking late and was, in fact, driving drunk. The young man killed in this incident had been driving home to his dorm from working a late shift on the weekend.

I met young Naoki at 2:30 AM, August 13, 2009. He was still very angry about his death and lamented that the young woman he holds responsible for the accident was never formally tested for drunk driving and was therefore never charged in his death. He showed me a glimpse of her in current life where he sees her as quite happy and settled with a husband and children. He does not think she deserves this happy arrangement. He stalks her and sometimes tries to hurt her or cause bad things to happen.

What he does not see is what I see; she is empty and guilt-ridden and though by all accounts she seems to be a happy person, this secret that she harbors affects her daily life and how she feels about herself for she has told no one about her past.

The following is Naoki's musings on life in his own words, as well as an account of our conversation together.

Shifting Gears

I loved cars, especially fast ones. I wouldn't own anything but a manual transmission as that's the only way to have complete control. There's a certain responsibility, you know, you have to pay attention closely. You can't be distracted by eating, talking or phones…you have to feel the car, see the road conditions, know how fast you are moving and be mindful of which gear it makes most sense in which to stay.

When you make a mistake, you know it immediately because the car will tell you in no subtle terms…it will whine if you downshift too quickly…sputter if the speed is too slow for the gear or simply leave it in gear with the motor running and the parking brake engaged and the car will lurch forward and die!

So, really, you must be aware of the car, shifting and surroundings. The rewards are more than worth it; you get to experience the thrill of the drive! Who cares that you are running an errand or going grocery shopping? I never owned a practical car in my entire, though short, life. Why? Because life *is* short.

I didn't care where I was going, I loved the trip and wasn't concerned about being late or early. I guess my death seemed tragic to many, yet, I felt it was a divine gift that I died behind the wheel of my beautiful Serena (that's what I had named her, my car). Like any good vehicle, she needed a first-class name. We perished together.

I know to you Americans that this sounds bad, but I would judge people very regularly based on the vehicle they owned. Of course, I do realize money is a constraint and people do the best they can with what they have…but even then, you do have some choices to make. How do you keep it; clean or dirty? Do you decorate it? Add any scents? It all says something about you.

It is my opinion that people who drive automatic transmissions are sheep; they drive through life never thinking about the shifts. When I was alive, there was nothing better than to hear the engine move through each gear. I don't think Americans are even aware of the automatic shifts that a car completes.

I sacrificed living in my homeland so that I could be educated in the Land of the Free and learn correct English. It was such a *sacrifice* to live in America. I am not being serious, though, because I really liked living in the USA, as long as it was temporary and I could return for visits.

People here are very different because of the freedoms they are afforded. They are also very conditioned and accept a great many things that people in my country would not. For example, if food tastes bad at a restaurant, my people will say so and send it back. I have had many dinners with my friends here and they will complain at the table about the food, yet, they will not tell the waitress. Also, it seems the Americans have the tendency to be passive-aggressive. Let me explain. If I am at an eatery and I need something to drink, I will ask…literally shout it out even if it annoys the help. I catch Americans clinking the ice in their glasses or moving cups to the edge of the table.

It is my observation that many Americans are like fatted cows grazing in a pasture unaware of anything happening around them…only taking notice when it's raining. They don't even notice that sleek sports car that just zoomed by.

I thought I had the world by the tail. I was fluent in three languages. My parents were very successful and our family enjoyed high social status. I would carry on the family name in an arranged marriage, though I would surely have known many lovers. I actually looked forward to that life. It was stolen from me by an American cow. She wasn't watching out for anyone else; she was selfish and not only took everything I had, she took away everything I was ever going to have. Sickening, but I watched my body as it was incinerated. I vowed revenge on the drunken cow, to reclaim my honor.

I watch her every day and every night. I stalk her. I try to let her know how much I hate her. I know she feels my presence. Sometimes I can move objects or break things if I'm in a mood for it. It's maddening that she dismisses her inner knowing, because if she did listen to it, it would tell her to be very afraid of what she cannot see. If I could kill her, I would. Not that I haven't tried, I just haven't been successful. Yet.

{At this point, Naoki left to go to check on the woman. He did not want to leave her alone. He wishes his constant presence in order to oppress her as much as possible. He wants to drain her energy and make her feel afraid and unhappy. He returned shortly and I joined him in the following conversation.}

Me: It takes a practiced ear to know when to shift; you have to listen carefully, right? You have to feel the whine in the motor. That's what you've said to me.

Naoki: Yes, I think that's exactly right. I really miss that.

Me: Do you think that you could look at your life from a different perspective? Perhaps, as with a manual transmission car, you have to pay attention to your life in the same ways?

Naoki: Sure, but I don't know exactly what you mean. I like cars and the idea that we can drive through life. I'd like to help a certain someone drive right over a cliff.

Me: Well, you know that you aren't living anymore. You have passed on to the Other Side and yet you have chosen to stay and torment the person you think is responsible for your death. Is that a fair depiction?

Naoki: Well, yes, I suppose so. I believe in revenge. I'm not a bad person...just don't cross me!

Me: I want you to step back from this situation. Instead of getting an up close and personal viewpoint, go to the aerial view. Do you think that you have help tormenting this woman?

Naoki: Unfortunately, no.

Me: Do you think that we, each and every person, have guardian angels helping to protect us?

Naoki: I'm not sure about that. Perhaps our ancestors look in on us from time to time…though I have not seen anyone.

Me: This woman that you torment, she has a guardian angel protecting her. All of the hate that you send to her doesn't reach her; her guardian angel is a shield.

Naoki: She knows when I am upset. She is afraid of me.

Me: Yes, that's true, even if she doesn't consciously know it. My question is, when the engine on your car reaches the rpm max for a gear and it begins to whine, what do you do?

Naoki: You shift the current gear to a higher one. Easy.

Me: When I look at your situation, when I listen, I hear that whine and I wonder why you haven't shifted gears. Go to the aerial view of your situation. Call your guardian angel to you. Come back to me when you are ready.

{Naoki's energy had been so strong that I was tired after our communication. I have not seen Naoki since this conversation. I will wait until he is ready. Until then, I keep the woman in my prayers and surround her with white light and protection.}

Rosalie

1990 in the Central Plains Region of the United States

I met Rosalie during the early morning hours of August 1, 2009. In my dream, I was riding a bicycle along a country road leading into a small town. I was enjoying the sights and sounds of an early afternoon in midsummer. As I began to see the small houses dot the landscape, I noticed one elderly lady in a wheelchair going to her mailbox at the end of her driveway. It surprised me greatly when her head lulled forward, eyes closed.

The wheelchair continued forward past the end of the drive and across the road right in front of me. I hopped off of my bike, caught the wheelchair and pulled the lady's hand from the control. Though her body was dying, I was witness as her soul departed. She was still seated when she looked around and then up at me in spirit and said, "Oh my goodness, how did this happen?" I had to smile.

Rosalie and I traveled to the Other Side together. The following is an account of our visit.

Light Superhighways

Rosalie stood up from her body, grasped my hands and we flew up and away into the cloudless blue sky. I had not been expecting that, especially from an elderly lady, though she had quite a sparkle in her eyes.

We were holding hands and flying through the sky at a pleasant clip when Rosalie looked over at me, smiling, and said, "I hope you don't mind, I just feel so happy to be out of that body. This is my favorite thing to do after I die...there's nothing quite like taking a lap around the world and watching all of the scenery just passing underneath. I really love it here but it was time to leave. I didn't expect to leave like that, except in some lifetimes when I just think about leaving and my soul immediately leaves. It happens. My old body was ready to rest and my soul has things to do."

So we flew on, taking in the sights, until at last we banked upward towards the gradually darkening sky. Soon we saw the blackness of space pinpointed with millions of colorful stars.

"I hope you don't mind," said Rosa, "but we're taking the long way, it is by far more beautiful."

I didn't mind one bit; it was surreal and wonderful. We continued until a very large black hole came into view. We were travelling very fast now and the star lights streamed by in colorful ribbons. We entered the darkness of the massive black hole and were swiftly transported through the blackness to a bright sky on the other side. We found ourselves falling gracefully into a strangely beautiful garden. We gently landed in between two very large trees. It felt timeless and calm. A thin, bearded man dressed in flowing robes was standing nearby. He was smiling at us.

"The Garden of Eden," said Rosa thoughtfully, "and we stand in between the Tree of Life and the Tree of Knowledge. I love this."

The man's lips parted in a cryptic smile as he offered us each a half of a dark-skinned fruit and half of a light-skinned fruit. Bright red juice dripped from our hands. Rosalie wasn't wasting any of it; she caught it in her mouth and it trickled down her chin. Her appearance had changed drastically from that of an old woman to a young girl with long dark hair. I began eating the small fleshy seeds contained within the red fruit. They were sweet and delicious but a lot of work to eat.

"That is a pomegranate," said the man who was Rosalie's guide as he gestured at the red fruit, "and the other is a fig."

Rosa smiled, "Your impression of Jesus is extraordinary, as is this version of the Garden of Eden, Tree of Life and the Tree of Knowledge."

"This is no version of the Garden, we are truly here. I thought to bring you back to the perceived beginning; many people's belief sustains this Garden as the beginning."

"Tell me which fruit is forbidden? If it is the pomegranate, then I am doomed already," said Rosa with a truly devilish smile. How quickly her face could change from angelic innocence to impious virtuousness.

"Truly, neither fruit is forbidden; knowledge and life should be partners and not enemies," said 'Jesus'. "Knowledge of good and evil is required in order to advance beyond ignorance; a state of ignorance always does harm. Bliss is the state yet to come after we rejoin with the Creator Source. Ignorance does not equal bliss."

"Why would the fruit of the Tree of Knowledge be forbidden in the sacred texts on Earth," asked Rosa.

"It is because to remove oneself from ignorance means to make a choice, even if that choice is forbidden by someone in authority. You must experience the inner dilemma of choosing – experience the good and the bad results. This is how we learn. Temptation is all around us, and it is our ability to make decisions that helps us to advance. Eve is often shunned as the perpetrator of Original Sin; truly she was the individual of stronger will and made the choice to experience instead of reside in a state of ignorance. It is because of Eve that man began the journey toward enlightenment."

I stood a little apart from 'Jesus' and Rosalie in the Garden of Eden in between the two massive trees. I could not believe I was here! It was a deeply spiritual and peaceful place. I had always imagined it would be so. I had always been upset with the proposition that women were responsible for mankind's supposed fall from grace. I had never believed that women were weaker than men. I began to understand more about choice and our responsibilities of choice.

I had trouble concentrating on the conversation as the form of 'Jesus' was simply too appealing. I was truly in awe. Sensing this, the 'Jesus' form morphed into a rather large snake right before my eyes and settled into the bough of the lowest branch of the closest Tree.

"Does this form suit you better," hissed the snake to me.

"Yes, I quite like it," I said. However, I wasn't sure I would watch this form any less than the previous one.

Rosalie was patiently waiting. "Are you here to tempt us, wicked snake," she asked.

If a snake could grin, then that is the expression I saw flash across its face.

"Perhaps you will be tempted to understand your next life in a different way because of what you will learn now," said the snake.

"What if I do not connect so well to the story of Adam and Eve? I remember a time when this story was considered brand new. I hearken to a time that is much earlier than Jesus' time," said Rosa.

With that, Rosa reached into the air and pulled at something that appeared as a thread from a piece of fabric. She plucked the shining string of light. The world around us blurred for a moment until settling in a world of darkness. Everything that had been, was gone. I was greatly confused.

Rosalie regarded me, understanding my bewilderment.

"We live in a world of light energy. Find the light strand that will take you to the place you want to go and then travel with it; it is almost instantaneous and can feel like the world around you shifts instead of the reality that you are traveling to that destination. It is very quick travel," explained Rosa.

I nodded, but of course, was still somewhat confused.

The snake was no longer present as a snake; indeed there was a person cloaked in purple that stood near to us in the dim firelight. The person, I knew, was Rosalie's guide in a different form yet again.

"Let me explain it in a different way," said the guide. "For example, when you smell a familiar fragrance from your past, the act of doing so can actually be the thread of light of which Rosa spoke. When you close your eyes, the time, place and even the memory that you perceive becomes reality. It is real, this place you have visited, and exists in time."

Again I nodded, though this time in somewhat further understanding. As I write this story, and indeed all of these stories, it is like I grasp a mental thread that takes me to the places I need to go or to the people I need to see in order to write.

"Why have you taken us from the Garden of Eden, which was a pleasant place, to the darkness of the Underworld," asked the guide.

"My thoughts are of the myth of Persephone, daughter of God Zeus and Goddess Demeter in ancient Greece," said Rosalie. "Kidnapped by Hades, God of the Underworld, she was forced to keep him company. He loved her, and though she did not love him, he waited. For many months she ate nothing and kept quietly to herself, taking no pleasure in any gift he gave to her. What she desired most, he could not give her.

"She missed her mother and the light of the sun. The only food that tempted her was the sweet pomegranate. Though she had no appetite, the red fruit was too much to resist and she ate four juicy seeds. Little did she know that anyone who ate anything in the Underworld would not be allowed to return to the living world. It was only through her mother's persistence and intervention to take her home again that a bargain was struck. Persephone was required to stay in the Underworld for four months of the year, based on the number of seeds she had eaten."

"What parallels do you see," asked the guide. Flecks of color and light swirled and jumped within the purple robes.

"Our time on Earth is like Persephone's time in the Underworld. Though we are not kidnapped, it may feel that way during our first few incarnations. Yet, we know within ourselves that it is our choice – just as Persephone knew that she was required to spend time in the Underworld for part of the year; we must also spend time on Earth. The choice becomes how we spend our time there. Persephone embraced her time in the Underworld and chose to be queen, ruling and making a huge difference for those around her during the time she was required to be there. Of course, we could simply complain about being here and miss our opportunities to help ourselves and others," stated Rosalie.

"We miss the Light but we are still nourished. To be separate from the Source is the most difficult undertaking," said the somber guide.

"The juicy seeds represent the sweetness of life that we can still enjoy knowing that eventually we will return in the proper timing to our true home that awaits us," said Rosa.

"Four months of challenge and difficulty and eight in Paradise…the sweet will follow whatever bitter may come, though you will experience sweetness in the most unlikely places as I'm sure that Persephone would tell us," said the guide.

I smiled, realizing that no one is wrong in their approach, whether it is within the bounds of religion or paganism or if it is mono or poly-deistic approach. The purpose is the same, to grow and be nourished and ultimately reunite with our Source. It is not the Source who controls how we are to advance, it our choice how we are to advance…in whatever manner we choose.

I take great comfort in knowing that I can travel to other places with the pulling of a thread of light…even if I don't stay in that moment, I can savor it while it lasts and then know it is time to move forward. Much more awaits us in the future than does in the past.

As I stood there, in the Underworld, with Rosalie and her guide, I knew that I could find my own way home without their assistance. I closed my eyes and sought the stratified energy that surrounded us. I reached forward in front of my chest and found the thread. It felt a bit sticky between my fingers.

I opened my eyes and thanked my hosts. I bade them farewell and tugged on the line. Everything around me shifted and I was at once standing in the middle of my bedroom. This is a true account of what I experienced…and I will never forget the message conveyed or the simplicity and directness through which we can travel with our minds.

9

Statements From Unconventional Visitors

Everything Is Energy

What if everything we thought we knew about time, space and dimensions turned out to be wrong? Well, wrong is a strong word and not quite right, but let's say that we haven't changed our initial thinking about these ideas for a very long time. Our laws of physics are still based on Isaac Newton's *Principia* published in 1687.

Newton's laws describe a physical world in which each particle of matter follows laws of movement; kind of like a machine. I always think of the inner workings of a clock; every cog and wheel has a precise job to do and it is very predictable.

What if we need to start thinking of this world, indeed our universe, in a different way? Perhaps our world is not set-up like a machine. Perhaps we need to expand our thinking to encompass some very different ideas.

I found the following stories to be enlightening and stimulating. I was not sure what to expect from these Visitors. In this chapter, I wrote the stories first and then wrote this introduction. I have been both surprised and pleased at the concepts contained herein. I honestly hope that these new ideas take hold in our current time. I'm certain that we are ready for something new. Just the fact that we are seeing so many new 3D movies makes me believe that we as a society are ready to view the world in a different way.

The main idea expressed in the following stories is that we need to understand that there is only one fundamental property of physics: energy. The secondary idea is that we, our minds, have an effect on this energy. Everything in this world, including us, is made up of energy. Everything we do and think is an energy exchange. Everything we say is an energy exchange. If you can believe that, at a quantum level, we are connected to everything and there are no boundaries between us, then you can start to see some major implications; we have way more control over ourselves and our surroundings than we ever thought before.

The Traveler
Any Time and No Time
Any Place and No Place

The heat rose in waves from the blacktop road. I was in the desert, seemingly alone. I wasn't alone, though, for someone had brought me to this place. He stood quietly across from me on the other side of the road. He was wearing worn-out blue jeans and boots but no shirt. His long brown and gray hair hung down past his tanned shoulders and was held back out of his eyes by a narrow leather headband.

Most notable to me was a long silver chain that hung around his neck with a small indiscernible symbol. It flashed in the brightness of the sun despite the fact that the man did not move. He has given me no name because names for him are too limiting...he is a traveler of worlds, times and places and prefers the simplicity of this form. For me, it is the morning of June 25, 2009. The following is a message from the Traveler in his own words.

Matter Doesn't Matter

We are all travelers. We don't need directions; we just go where we go. Ask yourself why you are where you are today? Do you want to be there? Maybe you do. Chances are that you don't. You're spending time doing what everyone else wants you to do...what your circumstances demand you to do. But life is about freedom and love.

You create and live in your own prison; you are the inmate and the guard. Once you're there for so long a time you don't want to leave because it is easy living. You have a defined space that you don't have to leave and it's comfortable. Being on the "outside" scares you. GOOD. It should scare you a little bit. That means you're sane. I worry, though, about those of you who are entirely happy – that means you are not challenging yourself and therefore you are not growing. Question this.

Do what it is in your nature to do, but by all means, EXPLORE. Go out of your comfort zone. This will help you to grow in ways you may not have imagined.

You can't live your life according to other people. You can't accept their issues as yours. You can't make another person happy if they are not happy with themselves. If you know how hard it is to change yourself or make changes in your own life, then you realize you cannot make another person change. There are so many people in this world, there IS someone for you. Don't stay with someone if you aren't happy, because chances are that they aren't happy with you. Sure, talk about it, see what you can come up with, but many times we just need to let people go in order to find their happiness – just as you go to find your own.

The energies that we carry with us morphs as we go through life according to our experiences and desires; sometimes we grow away from those whom we were once close with and sometimes we grow together. Either way, we are on a journey with our life companions seeking meaning. If we are not better people because of our companions, then question why you are with these people.

I know you've noticed my necklace. You can't tell what symbol hangs at the bottom, right? That's because it's different for each person and it changes as you go along... That's right, you have your own necklace and it changes to reflect what you are most insecure about and so therefore focus on. A lot of people see a cross or some religious symbol; this signifies a serious concern about what happens after death. I mean, if your choice is heaven or hell, you'd choose heaven over a lake of fire...who wouldn't?

This way of thinking is archaic. It is time to move beyond this, to leave the darkness of threats and move into the light of growth through personal choice. Maybe, if you think about it, Earth is the closest thing to hell you will ever know; choice providing the stage for the trials and tribulations you go through. The death-crossing is easy, like being reborn into freedom on the other side.

The real growth for humanity will happen when humans can think beyond death, beyond the limitations of a physical body, beyond the current seeming limitations of scientific knowledge - even to change that norm which you now consider "scientific". It is time to expand. You are only limited by yourself.

Close your eyes and imagine your own necklace. Tell me, what symbol do you see? Consider carefully, what changes do you need to make?

I will come again; travel to speak to you at the appropriate crossing of space and time. We have much to discuss.

The Faceless Being

Perpetual Timing
Crossroads of Your Life

I walk in a grey and desolate place in this dream. I know I am dreaming, yet, it is inter-dimensional in feeling. Truly it is December 4, 2009, but in this place it feels timeless. Fog swirls around, like I am caught in a cloud. I'm not sure what I'm standing on or even what surrounds me, so it is all very surreal, like being in a void of sorts.

I feel another presence join me; it is a shrouded figure standing in front of me. This figure is not frightening, but the form is constantly shifting in and out of existence. I look to see the face of this figure beneath the hood, yet, though there is substance, there is no face to be seen. I am not upset; rather, I am confused at what this could mean. A bodiless vibration of a voice speaks from the figure.

Observer and Observed

You see me, but you see no face because I am possibility...I am nothing to you and yet everything to you all at once. Possibility has no expectations, therefore, you as an observer do not know what to expect. Let me explain.

Nothing exists independently from anything else. There is only one physical fundamental entity: energy. All particles interact with each other by exchanging energy through quantum means. Everything we see and know and are, at the subatomic level and lower, dissolves into particle clouds. When we observe these particle clouds, we interact with them, changing their behaviors, forming the patterns that we expect to see.

Because we are only particles with consciousness that choose this reality, we can change this reality; we can change the expected or existing patterns into new patterns. This means that what we believe is so…if you believe you can change, even physically change, then you can.

Seeming miracles happen when people believe that the impossible becomes possible. This information is to give you hope. You must rearrange your thinking patterns in order to accept this information. It may take time to truly comprehend the implications that I speak of today. Let me continue.

The present timeframe is simply a shifting configuration of energy with probability communicated back and forth between the past and the future. This "present" time does not really even exist. As soon as you observe something, it, on a subatomic level, breaks up into an infinite number of possibilities, all of which come into existence at the same time. All of these possibilities exist simultaneously in parallel worlds or universes. All possibilities are playing out at the same time; however, you are unaware of their existence because you only perceive one universe at a time.

Ask yourself what you really want. Each one of your futures lies in a state of rest until it is awakened by the choices you make in your "present" timeframe.

If you do not like where your choices have led you thus far, then it is time to let go of your current perceptions, consider new possibilities, and allow a new perception to occur. Awaken the future that you want.

The Lightning Lady

Moment to Moment
The Place that You Are

The weather was calm and beautiful as I lay my head on the pillow on the evening of January 9, 2011. As I closed my eyes and drifted to sleep, I was conveyed to a tumultuous, foreboding world.

It sounded like a storm was coming. The wind tousled my hair as I stood outside on the soft grass. There were no structures around me, just an open field. It was very dark and I could see; the stars usually above me are hiding. Thunder rumbled in the distance and I began to see flashes of lightning on the horizon.

As the lightning comes closer, I begin to see a figure walking in the distance, illuminated only by the lightning strikes. Strangely, in the darkness of time between the strobe-like flashes, it seems that the figure leaps great distances, seemingly transported forward with the flash. I know the figure is walking at a steady pace and the jumps forward are a trick of the light, dark and time.

I sat on the ground as the first few warm drops of rain began to fall. I am lulled into a drowsy, even meditative state within my dream, and I know that this is a dream. I stretched out to enjoy this almost hypnotic state as I watched the light show flashing in all directions across the sky. Illuminated clouds were lit from within while streaks snaked in beautiful arcs and forks over the entire sky.

The figure I had seen walking is now lying next to me. It seemed that the previous flash of lightning brought her softly and instantaneously next to me, or perhaps it was a trick of the eyes. I hadn't realized she was there until I looked and saw her. She was a lovely ghost-like creature with long black hair. She seemed to be part of the night, comprised of the storm itself. Of her appearance, most notable were her eyes; they were alive with electricity.

She took my hand into her own. I felt her vibration humming with energy. She had no heartbeat, instead, there was a constant pulsation. It seemed she spoke through the vibration. I have written below an account of her words.

Sparks of Creation

Like a spark in the night, the words that issue out from us contain the capacity to create and destroy. Think about the actual words you are using in your daily life. Avoid saying things that can spark something destructive. For example, I've often heard people say, "Oh, my job is killing me" or "I would die to go to that concert," or "I am so sick and tired of everything, I could just kill myself". This is the beginning of the storm, when the winds begin to blow. This is how we set in motion the storms in our lives that can become major turning points. As you will see, human behavior mimics nature, as we are of nature and we are nature.

I have chosen this setting, time and place in order to demonstrate this principle. Think about storm clouds; though you cannot see inside them there is so much happening. Tiny particles in the cloud move around picking up positive or negative energy charges. The positive charged particles stay light and rise to the top of the cloud. The negative charged particles get heavier and collect at the bottom of the cloud.

Tension between particles becomes evident as more and more particles become charged; they divide into opposing groups within the cloud. Have you ever felt torn in this way within yourself; like you aren't sure what to do? You may go back and forth about feeling good or bad about a situation. You are not alone. These particles not only reside within you, but also around you in your aura and they can be influenced by those of whom you choose to surround yourself. Be careful of the company you keep.

Likewise if you view a group of people with opposing points of view, the division of the group is evident. The group will pull apart because the opposing ideas repel one another; yet, in the end, there is an inevitable power of attraction that draws them together. When the power of attraction draws them (or particles) together, anticipate heat and friction. When the heat and friction builds and becomes too great to contain, the particles expel their energy at each other, completing a path for electricity to travel through the air. This is the flow of electricity, of lightning. Lightning is created by the attraction between opposite charges.

As you are aware, a lightning strike is unpredictable, yet the signs can be read that it will happen. Thunder always accompanies lightning. When you were small, though, your parents probably told you not to fear the thunder; there is truth in this. Yet also know that thunder is a warning. You may hear thunder rumbling from far away before you actually see any lightning. Start to be aware of the rumbles around you and take preventative measures.

No one knows exactly what will happen when lightning forms. Sometimes it stays within and behind the clouds lighting them from the inside or it may form beautiful flashes across the sky. Sometimes it will strike the ground and shatter a tree or melt sand. The one matter is certain, that once the lightning discharges, the particles become neutral again, yet whatever destruction that has occurred, remains. You may feel this neutrality in the aftermath of a fight, the same way you can feel the softness in the air around you after the storm has finished.

When it has gone quiet, the question becomes, was the destruction actually bad? A tree struck down by lightning will put forth new growth from the base. Sometimes, in order to move forward in our lives, we must allow the destruction of our current situations. Think about the relationship or work situation in which you may be participating that you are unhappy with; perhaps you have not allowed the strike associated with the friction you are feeling to happen. I say "allow" because you do have control. The choice is always yours to make.

What are you afraid of? The change does not need to be violent; the strike may very well happen within you. It is the consideration of what has been said or done in the past and the drive of where you want to be and the change that you allow to happen within yourself will occur...it is the strike of conviction. It is the conviction that you are better than your current situation; the rift of particles within you needs to align and accept that you now choose something different.

Sometimes you have no choice. You may go to bed upset and thinking about your situation and how difficult it is and not know what to do... then, the next morning you awake and though you have not made a decision, it is almost as if one has been made for you. At once, you feel the shift; away from the negative and towards the positive. You must move away from stagnation and towards the current of change. You know what you must do.

Though it may be difficult, the choice is no longer before you as whether to stay in the current situation or to leave it. This is your guides stepping in and intervening on your behalf in order for you to avoid something that might take you far away from your correct life journey. Once the strike happens, there is no going back. Something old has been destroyed and it is up to you to create something new.

Consider those people and situations that cause you to be on guard; people you may dislike or with whom you may not get along. Ask yourself why there is friction. Do you see something of yourself in that person? Do you envy what they have? Do they want what you have? Many times, as you have seen, opposites attract. Think about that person or situation very carefully from outside yourself before you pass judgment.

If you allow the creation of dramatic situations in your life, first, ask yourself why. Drama keeps people interested in their lives, like a TV show; yet it detracts them from the path they are to follow. Know that you can "un-create" these situations and learn from the process...and be aware for the next time. This does not mean that you should deny your emotions; instead, ask yourself why you are feeling those emotions.

When you think about un-creating dramatic situations, know that along with the discharge of electricity, you should expect to hear some booming. Others may not be happy with your choices, but you are not here to please others; you are here in this place and time for a reason. If you make another person's life easier or better or even more interesting, then they will not want you to change and pursue your life's true purpose. Only you can free yourself.

I will leave you with this final thought; lightning is always jagged because it follows the path of least resistance. A strike is utterly unique and it can never be duplicated. It is quick and does not linger. Think of your life in this manner. If you seek out your true purpose, you will not fight your way through life; it will be natural and come easy to you. Your journey will never be exactly as anyone else's. There is no one in the entire universe like you; you are one of a kind. Spend your time wisely, be kind and live the happiest life possible.

Concluding Remarks
Making the Connections
There is no path to happiness; the path is happiness.
~Buddha

For the most part the World doesn't acknowledge the true existence of the Soul. If it is acknowledged, it is an intellectual indulgence based on logical arguments. I challenge you to understand that a "knowing" of something within yourself is authentic; it is intimate knowledge consciously one with the Source of All That Is. So, your head may not know exactly what your heart knows; however, it is wise to listen carefully when you feel some sensation in your heart...it is giving you direction based on the distinction of mental intellect versus soul knowing.

It is our challenge to bring the existence of the soul from an intellectual concept to a personal experience. The soul is not separate from the body; it does not reside within us. We are fused while on the Earth – body and soul as one. All matter is energy; our bodies and our souls, there should be no distinction between the two. Energy is all there is; it's all that we are. We are totally and fully connected not only within ourselves, but also to everything else and our Creator Source. There is nothing else. Once we understand this, we are able to recognize our wholeness, our process and feel the rightness or wrongness in our everyday decisions and actions.

Many of us grow up learning only of the existence of the rational and logical part of ourselves. The state of knowing that we feel without under-standing is summarily dismissed because it does not logically make sense in society as it is now. A way of being and knowing beyond logical under-standing is never truly addressed unless the concept is diminished in some way.

Take, for instance, a vivid dream; when you are asleep, it seems as real as any place you have ever visited. However, when you awake, the dream fades with hardly a trace. Consider that everything in that dream was made alive and sustained by your consciousness during sleep. When you awaken, that sustaining consciousness is removed, and because it becomes a fragment of memory it is discounted as something that your subconscious mind created out of the substances of your fears, hopes or worries.

Sometimes this is true...but sometimes it is not true. Sometimes the places that we visit in our dreams are as real as those we visit in our waking life. There is balance in everything. One extreme does not exist without the other being in existence. It is the duality of life.

It is our challenge to see our lives through the duality of our nature, through logic but employing your innate knowing. By itself, logic is sequential, causal, one-dimensional, trapped in the past or lost in the future; it is the temporal world of a mortal.

By itself, the knowing of the Soul is holistic, ever present in the moment, multi-dimensional and simultaneous; it is the timelessness of life force and essence of all.

This book is a message and reminder that in this moment you can go beyond the worries, hurts, dreams, expectations and anxieties of your ego, and tune into your ever-present, satisfied and blissful soul. Logic and knowing together will afford us an authentic, positive and relevant, deeper understanding and meaning of our personal lives, from whatever background you have or spiritual path you have chosen to travel. The choice is always yours.

Acknowledgments

Transitions: Accounts of the Soul's Journey is a book of dream encounters. Each word is my true experience. I have always experienced a vivid dream life, yet when I began to have terrifying dreams complete with names and dates, I began to worry that I was losing my sanity. It seemed that I was witnessing events that had actually happened.

It is disturbing to wake up in a panic because you feel that your legs have been amputated or maybe not be able to breathe because you are sharing the experience of someone who is drowning. It took several years of sleeping pills and alcohol abuse before I was open to accept help.

It just happened one day that I felt drawn to a very peaceful feeling bookstore called Inner Path and met someone who changed my life. I saw her talking with someone at the counter and knew that I had to talk to her. Somehow, I knew she could help me with my dreams.

This woman happened to be a Spirit Artist. I had never heard of a spirit artist before. Her name was Ms. Shirley Culver and she drew my energy in many colors during our session without speaking a word. It became apparent to her that I needed some serious help as I was surrounded by spirits and other energy beings in the picture... all seeking my attention. My own energy was more connected to the Other Side than the world in which I was living. Shirley asked me a few pointed questions and I immediately broke down in tears. She could see and show me on paper the situation with which I was dealing; I had found someone who understood.

Shirley was the first person who saw what was happening and helped me to start looking at my situation differently. She helped to alleviate my fear and sleep better at night. She introduced me to Jacquelyn (Jacki) Madison, an RN and Spirit Worker who took me under her wing and helped me to understand the many different sides of what I was experiencing. Together Shirley and Jacki helped me to realize the opportunity that lay before me. Indeed, we discovered that I was not losing my mind at all. I had been experiencing visitations from people who had crossed over and wanted to have their stories written and communicate with the living.

I owe a debt of gratitude to Shirley and Jacki for their tireless and continued efforts on my behalf. They are both incredibly gifted and talented individuals and I would not have been able to walk this journey without their sage advice. It is fair to say that I would not be the person that I have become without them. Thank you will never be enough.

During the years I have worked on this book, my sweetheart, Jay, has given me more help and support than I had any right to expect. Beyond his endless patience, his willingness to drop everything and read when I needed his opinion, and his frankness and extreme thoughtfulness, he has shown me wonderful constancy and understanding.

I would also like to thank my parents and my sister for their great indulgence into the realm of possibilities that this book introduces. Your support and acceptance of me and my ideas is a testament to how much you love me. Thank you for allowing me the freedom of an open mind.

To my daughter, I must convey my gratitude for her willingness to allow me to work uninterrupted. Homework, lacrosse and friends all require much attention and she understood my dedication to finishing this book in a timely manner.

For her warmth, her directness and her careful reading of my manuscript, thanks to my good friend Martina Wickizer.

I'm grateful to Chris, Justin and several of the store team-members of Inner Path in Greenwood, Indiana for their support of this project early on in the process as well as continued support with the promotion of this book. Annie, I'm glad to have met you at Inner Path. You encouraged me to publish *Transitions* and showed me your book; *A Butterfly in the Garden* to prove to me that it could be done. Thank you! For those of you who may be interested, please visit http://godsigninstitute.com.

I'm profoundly in Marilene Isaacs' debt for the valuable role she played as I worked to bring this book into being. Her foresight and recommendations were invaluable and much appreciated.

Michael Dennis, I appreciate your generous involvement and your many thoughtful suggestions and ideas. I wish you only the best as you continue your career as an experienced author with many successful books, including *Morning Coffee with God* and *God's Many Mansions*.

I would be remiss if I did not mention the people who started me on this path of understanding; those of you who introduced me to new concepts that made true sense to me – you helped me on my Path.

Jack, though you are on the Other Side now, your patience and musings about energy and crystals taught me that everything has a voice if we listen.

Debbie and Janet, your selflessness and true awareness is a light to others. Your store, New Age People in Indianapolis, is a beacon to help many along in their Paths, including me.

Mary O., you exerted your wonderful influence without even knowing it...you introduced me to Reiki and will forever by my Reiki Master. I continue to use this gift you altruistically gave to me when I had nothing to give to you but friendship.

Anara, Child of the Stars, bless you for sharing your belief in Other Worlds and Other Beings. I will never forget how free I felt when I first considered this concept with you. Thank you for opening my eyes.

To Elisabeth, whom I called Hyssop for ever so long until I truly listened, my eternal gratitude is yours. Our journey together continues happily as long as your patience at my wandering ways endures.

Finally, for their creativity and professionalism, thanks so much to the editing and publishing team that made this project transpire so smoothly.

About The Author

Guinevere was born in a small town in Indiana. She was educated at Indiana University in Bloomington where she received a B.A. in 1996. She went to San Francisco and earned her certification to teach English as a Second Language, traveling then to Japan, working and living there from 1996-2003. She experienced various occupations in teaching as well as marketing and business development. In 2004 she earned a post-graduate degree in policy analysis from Murdoch University located in Perth, Western Australia. After returning to the United States, she co-founded a small consulting company and resides in Indianapolis, Indiana with her daughter. She may be contacted at Guinevere@GuinevereMassee.com.

For Further Information

Shirley Culver / Energy Artist

Shirley was the first person to recognize the root of my nightmares and explained how I could resolve that issue. Energy patterns are in a constant state of change. There are many factors that affect your energy, such as emotions, nutrition, environment and genetics. Contact Shirley if you'd like to know more about your own energy patterns. She visualizes these patterns and then does personal drawings of what she sees. Additionally, Shirley provides interpretation & recommendations for moving the energy patterns into a more healthy flow.

Visit Shirley's site for more information on her work as well as her contact information: www.energydrawings.com

Jacquelyn (Jacki) Madison / RN and Energy Worker

Jacki worked with Shirley in order to train me to recognize what was happening and better deal with the changes in the most correct way. It was through our few sessions that I was able to stop the alcoholism and drug addiction to sleeping pills. Not everything that happens to us is something we can explain; sometimes it takes someone else who has seen the situation before to tell you what is happening. This was my circumstance. I did not think that speaking to the dead was possible; I was wrong. Now that I have accepted that fact, I communicate regularly with many interesting souls.

I no longer accept the impossibilities that seem to exist, and by doing so, I open the possibilities in life.

For more information, please contact Jacquelyn directly at: jmadison@ etczone.com

Marilene Isaacs / Gifted Psychic, Medium and Energy Worker

Marilene lives in Indianapolis, Indiana in a beautiful 17-sided round house, which also serves as the headquarters for the Center of Peace, where clients visit Marilene. She has earned world renown for her psychic gifts and special abilities to help her clients. I became acquainted with Marilene in 2006, seeking her advice and also taking a few of her classes. Her guidance helped to clarify several of my life decisions. Marilene is a well known radio and television personality who has hosted and produced many of her own series.

Visit Marilene's website for further information: www.centerofpeace.com

www.ingramcontent.com/pod-product-compliance
Lightning Source LLC
LaVergne TN
LVHW011229080426
835509LV00005B/405